A House in the Country

A House in the Country

The Second Home from Cottages to Castles

by Mary Gilliatt

Photographs by Brian Morris

Hutchinson of London

HUTCHINSON & CO (*Publishers*) LTD.
3 *Fitzroy Square, London W*1

London Melbourne Sydney Auckland
Wellington Johannesburg Cape Town
and agencies throughout the world

First published 1973

This book has been set in Baskerville, by Flarepath Printers Ltd.,
St. Albans, Herts, and printed by offset litho on cartridge paper by
Ebenezer Baylis & Son Ltd., Leicester,
and bound by Wm. Brendon of Tiptree, Essex

ISBN 0 09 111610 4

For D'Arcy and John
who first convinced me of the charms of country houses
and for Roger who made them possible.

Contents

Acknowledgements

In any book of this sort one inevitably relies heavily on the direction and help of friends. I am particularly indebted to Dr and Mrs Roger Bannister, Mrs Caroline Conran, Mr and Mrs Gerald Cookson, Sir Robin and Lady Darwin, Mrs Marston Fleming, Mr Billy McCarty, Mr and Mrs Christopher Murphy, Mr and Mrs William Scott, Mrs Stuart Wallace, Professor and Mrs John Walton and Mr Paul William White. I must also thank all those owners of houses who so kindly let us photograph and entertained us at what was often, but inevitably, an inconvenient time, and Vogue and Woman's Journal for permission to use photographs previously used in articles.

I am equally grateful to Mr and Mrs King of Rattlesden for all their care of our own house, and to Mr and Mrs Everitt of Tostock who first made the whole venture feasible. And lastly, but by no means least, I would thank Mrs Judy Lance for her advice and forbearance which meant—and means—so much.

Introduction

In England alone, there are now supposed to be almost a million second homes. This is a statistic one can hardly credit in a time of such chronic under-housing, but if the situation can be said to hold comfort for anyone other than the fortunate owners, it must be for those concerned with the problems of conservation and environment. For clearly a great many buildings which would otherwise have been left to rot, are now being rehabilitated, often very sensitively.

Moreover, although there is inevitable initial resentment if not positive dislike of weekenders on the part of country people, it must be remembered that the infiltration could well be the salvation of rural Britain. Eyes jaded by urban rush and sprawl are yet quick to notice any despoliation, any deviation from that rural charm and disorder which they have been at such pains and such expense to acquire. Part-time country dwellers are often, although by no means always, more conservation-minded than their full-time neighbours. In any event, one good conspicuous conversion in a village can often set standards rising, just as in towns a single refurbished house in a decrepit terrace will often, in time, raise the character of the neighbourhood.

Of course it can be argued that to set standards rising in a village, means that prices are set rising as well, which has the corollary of not only driving the real villager out, but of changing the often haphazard agricultural character of the place to at best one of self-conscious

'. . . a small dwelling less in size than the house of a farmer, with no more than three bedrooms . . .'

rurality. This is true. But if the alternative is brash speculative development, a string of dreary local authority housing, and a rash of superficial modernities in the way of paints and accessories which bear no relation to true modernising, the newcomers are to be preferred. Then, too, weekenders can help support a battling village store rapidly losing custom to the local supermarket, provide occasional domestic jobs and do much to revive a flagging village economy.

Three or four years ago, Elspeth Huxley pointed out with some truth that "inside every Englishman is a villager struggling to get out with such success that scarcely a dank hovel remains in the remotest hamlet that has not now been turned into a gadget-happy country cottage, a Jaguar resting where the privy used to be". It is a meretricious, not entirely agreeable

picture of twentieth century country life and has been much quoted, but at least a good deal of memorable domestic architecture has been saved in the process, and for that matter, an integral part of Britain and Ireland.

This book really started out to be a review of these revamped cottages with the hope that it might possibly inspire more people to undertake the same exercise to such effect. Its aims were to explore the phenomenon of restoration; to record the infusion of urban enthusiasm into the countryside, and at the same time to give some practical advice on conversion and building.

I wanted to photograph and record these propped-up, rehabilitated, redecorated and often radically altered cottages. But in the process I found it very difficult to keep to the subject. The true cottage, as John Woodforde pointed out in his extraordinarily interesting *The Truth About Cottages* (Routledge & Kegan Paul), is a small dwelling less in size than the house of a farmer, with no more than three bedrooms. A house built originally, he might have added, for the occupation of a rural labourer or a craftsman. For many families looking for a bolthole, a place where the children can have at least a chance of learning about the country, this is too small. Their search, and consequently my search, began to stretch itself into barns and windmills, granaries and deserted village schools, derelict railway stations and chapels, discarded farmhouses and rectories, Peel towers and Norman keeps, decrepit orangeries and pavilions, ruined follies and castles, not to mention the new houses that they built either out of aesthetic duty (in the belief that anyone who could afford to should build at least one house in a lifetime), because they found their perfect but houseless site or because all else failed to suit them.

The net spread from the British Isles to Ireland. Far from being a parochial book on modern cottage decoration it became an illustrated essay on a new aspect of British country living; a much more general review of what I could only think of as the other house, so varied were the individual components.

Second houses, are not necessarily models of decoration. Usually they are holiday houses, houses for relaxation, chosen more for their site, position, amenities and their external aesthetic qualities. This does not mean that there are few of decorational merit. Some of them manage to combine all the virtues and are clearly the owners' most treasured possession. But it does mean that they demand a treatment—more often than not curtailed by finances—involving a fusion of practicality and comfort, simplicity and gaiety, which is seldom so much in evidence in a main house.

They have to be sturdy enough to withstand enormous influxes of visitors of every age, and possibly periods of letting to less than careful tenants, as well as periods of absence. They must be spare enough to curtail temptation to break-in when they are standing empty; well-planned enough to make life as easy when in residence as is possible. Often they are the natural receptacles for cast-off furniture, the obvious place for the cheap, the cheerful, the expendable.

Naturally there are exceptions. For some people the county house is the prized house, the cosseted house, the adventurous house, the place in which they will eventually spend all their days—and occasionally in this book it is the house in which they do spend most of their days, or the house that has been retired to. In these houses there is often a greater degree of formality and care.

Whatever the case, I have tried to give a cross-section of examples which will give as wide a picture as it is possible to give of the network of ideas now current, and of practices being pursued.

For ease of reference, I have grouped the houses into sections on Cottages and Farmhouses, Conversions, Comfortable Country, Castles, Towers and Follies and The Modern House. This seemed to me the most logical, for although location plays a substantial part in building (houses by rivers or the sea, or right in a village dictate their own rules, just as stone houses need different treatment than, say, lathe and plaster; and goodness knows, there are enough regional variations in Britain to fill several books), I found it difficult looking through the assembled photographs of interiors to say with any certainty that this house must be in Suffolk or that in Gloucestershire, this in Scotland or that in Western Ireland.

This, I think, has less to do with late twentieth century taste and that universal style which is so often criticised for taking away the last vestiges of idiosyncrasy, than the common denominator of houses provided, however wistfully, for the particular purposes of leisure, pleasure and country living.

Cottages and Farmhouses

I link cottages and small farmhouses together here because there has for a long time been a certain amount of confusion as to when the one merges into the other. In fact the word cottage has become a fairly generic term for almost any small house, and the old half-timbered, or flint or stone houses of yeoman farmers have been called cottages for so long that we are inclined to forget that the true cottage was more hovel than house and remained so until the 1770s.

True, the great rural building period in England took place between 1550 and 1660 before timber became in short supply towards the middle of the seventeenth century when huge quantities were taken for ship building and iron smelting, but in spite of this, a cottage in the sixteenth and seventeenth centuries meant either a one-room structure of mud with reeds laid on branches for a roof, or else a weak timber structure with the framework filled in with mud. The small but substantial oak-framed houses that survive in such numbers today, were by no means mere cottages to their original inhabitants. They probably had only two bedrooms, but they belonged to men of means like sheep farmers, merchants, weavers and tradesmen, who, for the most part, owed their prosperity to the wool business.

An Essex clergyman called Harrison recorded in 1577 that 'Never so much oke hath been spent in a hundred years before as in ten years of our time. For everyman almost is a builder, and he that hath

Bind it together with iron when it loosens; stay it with timber when it declines...'

bought any small parcel of ground, be it ever so little. will not be quiet till he have pulled downe the old house, if anie were there standing, and set up a new after his own device.' Unhappily, the fleece that was proving so golden to the yeoman class, reduced the need for farm labour so that many of the poor had no option but to become squatters, putting up wretched shacks on the outskirts of villages which were as much frowned upon by the then Parish authorities as caravan camps are today.

The destitution reached such a pitch that in 1589, Queen Elizabeth signed an act against the Erecting and Maintaining of Cottages, which directed that in future no cottage was to be built unless four acres of land went with it. The land need not be adjoining the cottage, but could be in strips in the common field. As it turned out, so many ex-

ceptions were allowed by the authorities that the act caused only a partial disruption in hovel-building, and in 1663 the Worcestershire Quarter Sessions sent out circular letters to the justices about the great number of cottages being erected, reminding them that it was 'a work of as great concernment as any we know, for the great neglect of late in this particular has caused this county to abound with more poor than any county we know of'.

By the eighteenth century, agricultural and other industries were more productive, and the beneficiaries of this new prosperity began another building boom. All sectors from the middle and professional classes upwards were building according to their means; local builders had access to the latest pattern books and had no difficulty at all in producing the regular-looking houses that everyone seemed to want; houses with symmetrically-placed front doors and equally symmetrical sash windows. Timber-framed houses were out of fashion and were often cladded, the more to resemble fashionable Georgian, and in the South-East in particular there was a craze for an ingenious nail-hung tile which could make a timber-framed house appear to be built of brick.

But the rural labourers of the time lived in buildings with no such graces. The average cottage consisted of one room only with perhaps a lean-to shed. Farmhouses on large properties were rent-producing since they were needed for the tenant-farmers made necessary by the new Enclosure Acts, and it was therefore a good investment for the landlord to build handsome farmhouses. It was a great deal less attractive, to build, or even repair, cottages for the landless labourers.

By the middle of the century, in the current climate of incipient liberalism, enough voices were being raised in protest against the accepted view of the poor as useful but insensate rabble to start various landlords rivalling each other in the benevolence of their building programmes. Nathaniel Kent's book, 'Hints to Gentlemen of Landed Property' published in 1775, was nevertheless the first publication to contain plans for model cottages, and even then, he pointed out that there was little use in labourers' dwellings being fine or expensive, since all that was required was a 'warm, comfortable, plain room for the poor inhabitants to eat their morsel in, an oven to bake their bread, a little receptacle for their small beer and provisions, and two wholesome lodging apartments, one for the man and his wife and another for his children.'

The first architectural book devoted entirely to cottages was produced by John Wood, architect of the Royal Crescent in Bath, and he made the point that if cottages were to be built in pairs, the inhabitants could be of use to each other in cases of sickness or accident. Wood also pointed out that the windows of main rooms should receive their light from the South or East so that they would always be 'warm and cheerful'. This was a much more radical suggestion than it appears now, since up until that time the idea still lingered in the country that the South wind brought the plague and that therefore principal rooms should face North, which is presumably the reason why so many British houses face the wrong way round.

Many late eighteenth century landlords however, were convinced that cottage building could only be attractive if it was planned according to picturesque principles. To many, the half-broken-down hovels that were so usual a sight over the countryside were picturesque enough in their own right, but in the days when people could actually advertise for, and employ, *soi-disant* hermits to live picturesquely in their parks, this was not enough, and from the 1780s, designs for picturesque cottages appeared constantly in the pattern books.

The unpleasant realities of the majority of cottages failed to deter the rich from the idyll of the cottage as providing all contentment and the healthy, virtuous life, and by the end of the century 'cottages of gentility' as Robert Southey sneeringly called them, or cottages for the gentry were familiar sights. The cottage was now dignified in both size and concept. James Malton wrote his *Essay on British Cottage Architecture* in 1798, and besides being a treatise on the picturesque, it was also calculated to persuade his readers that his cottages would make very pleasant retreats for themselves. He described his ideal rural dwelling as 'a small house, of odd irregular form, with various harmonious colouring, the effects of weather, time and accident, the whole environed with smiling verdure, having a contented, cheerful, inviting aspect, and a door open to receive a gossip neighbour, or weary, exhausted traveller. There are many indescribable somethings that must necessarily combine to give a dwelling this distinguished character. A porch at entrance; irregular breaks in the direction of the walls, one part higher than the other; various roofing of different materials, thatch particularly, boldly projecting; fronts partly built of brick, partly weather-boarded, and partly brick-nogging dashed; casement window lights, are all conducive and constitute its features.'

Jane Austen is a particularly graphic witness to the upstaging of the cottage. Uppercross Cottage in *Persuasion* had been a farmhouse of little consequence until the marriage of young Charles Musgrove when it was 'elevated into a cottage for his residence'. And 'with its verandah, French windows and other prettinesses, was quite as likely to catch the eye as the more consistent and considerable aspect and premises of the Great House, about a quarter of a mile further on'.

Barton Cottage in *Sense and Sensibility* had four principal bedrooms and two garrets and though small was comfortable and compact. 'But as a cottage it was defective, for the building was regular, the roof was tiled, the window shutters were not painted green, nor were the walls covered with honeysuckles. A narrow passage led directly through the house into the garden behind. On each side of the entrance was a sitting room, about sixteen foot square; and beyond them were the offices and the stairs. . . . It had not been built for many years and was in good repair.'

But like many of us with new country acquisitions, Mrs Dashwood had great plans for Barton. 'Perhaps in the Spring, if I have plenty of money, as I daresay I shall, we may think about building. These parlours are too small for such parties of our friends as I hope to see often collected here; and I have some thoughts of throwing the passage into one of them, with perhaps a part of the other, and so leave the remainder of the other for the entrance; this, with a new drawing room which may be easily added, and a bed chamber and garret above, will make a very snug little cottage. I could wish the stairs were handsome. But one must not expect everything, though I suppose it would be no difficult matter to widen them. I shall see how much I am before-hand with the world in the Spring, and we will plan our improvements accordingly.'

Plus ça change, plus c'est la même chose. Today, cottages and farmhouses, bought, on the whole, to be improved, are staple weekend and holiday fare. The myth of the joys of cottage life put forth by eighteenth and nineteenth century sentimentalists has been forcibly turned into reality by urban citizens determined to secure and enjoy some measure of rural pleasure while it can still be obtained. Many farm-workers and villagers, after years of living in ancient, crumbling structures with the privy at the bottom of the garden, are only too glad to be lured away by the superior heating and sanitation promised by council housing and speculative development. This factor, together with the centralisation of agriculture so that more and more acres are farmed from a central point by the big landlords, has meant that there are a plethora of labourers' cottages and small farmhouses to be bought.

Indeed, as I mentioned in my introduction, this injection of urbanism into the countryside, or at any rate, urban ideals of bucolic delights, though naturally resented at first, might well result in the aesthetic saving of the landscape, or at least what landscape as is left. To revive old buildings and gardens, and yet retain their character and essence as it were, certainly demands money, but equally, it needs imagination and knowledge and above all sensitivity.

The most important point to remember when rehabilitating an old farmhouse or cottage is to be guided by the structure of the house itself. Exaggerate the natural ingredients by all means; regenerate the simplicity of rural decoration, pare away the inessentials, try to distinguish between the bogus, the fake and the truly traditional; and be as honest as you can. Perhaps one could do a great deal worse than remember Ruskin's sentimental adage: Watch an old building with anxious care; guard it as best you may, and at any cost, from any influence of dilapidation. Count its stones as you would the jewels of a crown. Set watchers about it, as if at the gate of a besieged city; bind it together with iron when it loosens; stay it with timber when it declines. Do not care about the unsightliness of the aid—better a crutch than a lost limb; and do this tenderly and reverently and continually, and many a generation will still be born and pass away beneath its shadow.'

Because as a nation we have had the extreme good fortune never to have been plundered by an invading army, nor indeed, to have suffered a land invasion since the Normans, and because as a result we are in possession of so many buildings in a fair state of preservation which go back three, four, and five hundred years and sometimes longer, we would seem to have a particular responsibility to show consideration to the past, to learn from it, and at the same time to provide for the future.

The cottages and farmhouses that I have photographed for this section have all been patient rehabilitations of wrecks, or near wrecks. It is an encouraging collection.

Hall in the author's home in Suffolk

14

A Pair of Labourers' Cottages in Suffolk

This pair of half-timbered labourers' cottages set full on to a narrow overgrown Suffolk lane would please any travel poster designer. Thatched and covered with rambling roses which manage to grow through the upstairs windows and even through the thatch, it possesses splendid ingredients like a galleried hall and upstairs windows that start at floor level. It has been so skilfully modernised that one hardly notices it, but it was converted by Robert and Diana Banks almost single-handed, for they did a great deal of the building, decorating and structural work themselves.

Robert Banks bought the cottages before he was married and worked on them in weekends and whenever he had any spare hours. When he first found them they were tumble-down, derelict, thoroughly depressing. But he had the wit to see their possibilities, and the skill to draw them out. The conversion took several years, and he and his wife worked on them, improving them, whenever they had the time or the money.

The result is very cheering for all would-be converters who are willing to do the work themselves. It is traditional without being hackneyed, gay without being garish. Because the two cottages are treated as one there is a good deal more space than is normally associated with buildings of this type. The galleried hall was achieved by removing part of the first floor and adding a balustrade. To the right there is a dining room painted dark brown, to the left a white sitting room and beyond that a cinnamon-coloured study stacked with shelves for books and Mr Banks's collection of treen. The kitchen is built out behind the hall and dining room. And the upstairs bedrooms ramble along, one leading into another, and each with a more sloping floor than the last.

Left: *Galleried hall*
Top: *Study*
Above: *Main bedroom*

A Brick and Tile Farmhouse in Hampshire

When David Gunn bought his early eighteenth century brick and tile farmhouse in Hampshire a few years ago, it was written-off as a near hopeless case on the estate agents' books. He started to revive it as much as he could himself, cured the worm and rot, and made it reasonably habitable for a bachelor. Then he married, and together he and his wife made it not only habitable but practical and covetable as well.

As you go through the present front door (they plan to replace the main entrance with another more idiosyncratic one at the side of the house) you are confronted quite unexpectedly with a large, cool sitting room full of flashes of colour against an expanse of pammented floor and a mixture of old furniture and modern classics: chairs by Eames and Jacobsen and astonishingly good pieces designed by Mrs Gunn's late husband, the architect Raymond Wilson.

Fabrics are fresh; black and white linen on one sofa, green and yellow cushions on another. Through open doors you get a quick impression of subtle blue-green walls in a small television room cum study, and terracotta walls, heaped bookshelves, a piano, and white Saarinen furniture in the dining room. Further exploration shows that the dining room, as indeed the kitchen next door, open out on to a terrace, punctuated here and there with terracotta pots, which verges in its turn on to grass and ponds and hayfield and woods.

Beyond the sitting room is a long hall, paved and terracotta-walled with a new staircase leading up to the bedroom floor, bright with rich colour and views over the greenness of the valley.

It is small and compact and easy to run, though the general feeling is of airy space. But the Gunns have great plans for the outbuildings. The long barn is going to be made into a huge playroom cum party room with a long study or work room upstairs. The barn nearest the house will house an indoor, or at least a covered swimming pool, since they hope to dig out the walls leaving the supporting piers. And the lean-to at the side of the house will be an extra spare room and rose-clambered porch for the new front door. Behind the house, yet another barn is being made into a separate small house for guests who will then be welcome for as long as they like to stay.

Looking at the photographs of the exterior it is difficult to see that in fact the far right hand side of the front, which now houses the kitchen and the main bedroom, is completely new. This subtle blending was achieved with the help of some exactly matching bricks. And the whole complex of farm buildings with their totally new usages is a model in its way of what to do with neglected outhouses.

Above: *Dining room/study*
Right: *Hall staircase*

Left: *A corner of the sitting room*
Below: *Another view of the sitting room*

A Farmhouse in West Suffolk

I am prejudiced in writing about this particular house since it is our own. When we first found it, overgrown, over-modernised and jerry-converted, it had little to commend it except its size, its position, its price and the possibilities inherent in its basic ingredients. It was originally two cottages: one, which must have been a small Elizabethan farmhouse scheduled as an ancient monument of a rather lesser grade, the other Victorian and joined to the original at right angles.

It was dark, damp, unkempt, and full of irritating added details, such as electric fires sunk in where the fireplaces should have been, curly wrought-iron door furniture and mock lead-paned metal framed windows. With the aid of some sympathetic local architects, John Abbott and Ian Hamilton-Penney, we set to work to strip the floors to reveal the old brickwork beneath, to pare away the electric fires and backing to reveal the original fireplaces, and to take down the wall either side of the main chimney breast to make a much larger living space with a central fire. Since one side smoked we decided that the best policy was to raise the level to waist height and use the space underneath for storing and drying logs.

Common safety dictated that we pull down the staircase which was as precipitous as a ladder and a great deal more rotten than any ladder has a right to be, and replace it with a new set of stairs set at a more comfortable angle. We turned the old kitchen, which was badly placed and too low, into a utility room, cloakroom and small extra bedroom, and enlarged the old scullery to make a new kitchen-breakfast room. And we made an extra bathroom by slicing off one end of a large bedroom.

We got rid of the worst of the windows and replaced them with simple wood casements; threw away the wrought-iron excrescences everywhere, and substituted simple traditional East Anglian latches; bricked up the odd door, opened others, and opened one blocked-up window in the hall (which had been filled in when the lean-to scullery was added) right down to the ground so that light poured in from the windows of the breakfast room beyond.

For the rest, we held together the more crumbling plaster walls with wallpaper, continued the brick floors over the whole of the ground floor area, and kept plain polished wide elm planks upstairs, adding rugs where necessary. Because the new staircase looked a little brash against the beams and ancient curving walls, I decided to exaggerate it even more and stain it red, which at least relieves it of its post-war utility air. We continued the linking red by staining the bookshelves in the sitting part of the main living area the same colour, and staining equally the new supporting beams on the kitchen ceiling.

Because the main living room/dining room was so dark and lowering, we decided to lighten it cosmetically by painting the beams white and the plaster in between a nutmeg brown. We left beams in the hall, on the staircase wall and on the

landing in their natural state, but painted the plaster ochre, and one North-facing bedroom we coloured a cheerful tangerine.

The furniture is a mixture of seventeenth century, rustic nineteenth century, Art Nouveau and eclectic modern. That is to say, our twentieth-century examples range from a specially designed pair of sofas by Paul William White, to Italian Magistretti, 'UP' and Sacco chairs, with a variety of brightly painted pop pieces in between. Accessories: paintings, china, objects, are mainly nineteenth century, and we find the house a good receptacle for various collections of affecting Victorian farewell scenes, and mementoes testifying to the power of Victoria's Empire.

Since the windows were small I put up fabric blinds instead of curtains to allow in the maximum light, and we kept colours warm and lively, as we are only too well aware that in England anyway the sun does not always shine.

Top: *Kitchen/breakfast room*
Below right: *Dining room*
Below: *Staircase*

Above: *Bedroom*
Left: *View of the sitting room*
Below: *Another bedroom*

A Somerset Farmhouse in Cotswold Stone

When William Scott, the painter, and his wife Mary, decided to look for a house in Somerset they spent a great deal of time searching for exactly the sort of building that they wanted. The list of necessities was precise: it had to be small enough to be easy to maintain, large enough to be able to put up their family when necessary. It had to have outbuildings with at least one that was suitable for a studio. And they wanted a long view. When they finally stumbled across Bennett's Hill Farm one day, they knew it was exactly what they had formulated in their minds, but the house with its marvellous grouping of barns and farmyard, was almost a ruin.

Undeterred, they set to work to restore it, and turn the largest barn into a studio. Some walls were in a good enough state to be kept as they were, others had to be refurbished or entirely rebuilt. They opened up a huge living room on the ground floor reached through an airy hall, with a new staircase built-up against an ancient, whitewashed wall. Beyond the living room they built a terrace to take full advantage of the sun and the sweep of view over miles of verdant Somerset country to the White Horse Vale in the distance. Behind the living room, their son Robert Scott designed them a spacious, functional kitchen with every possible convenience, warmed by the good-looking wooden units, earthenware, and rush matting on the stone floor.

But the most remarkable thing about the house is the precise and careful detailing. Furniture, objects, paintings, are placed with an eye so accurate that each little grouping resolves itself into a still-life of its own. The white stone floor in the living room was hewn from a local quarry, and is juxtaposed with the white walls and the deep recesses of the doors that show the massive thickness of the walls. The lines and planes that are so extraordinarily revealed become a subject for contemplation. In fact these sudden revelations are not really so very extraordinary. If the house is the natural extension of the ego, then how much more is a painter's house the extension of his paintings? The whole house becomes his work.

Facing page—Above: *Kitchen from the living room*
Below left: *Kitchen*
Below right: *Living room*
Left: *Scott sculpture*
Below: *Main bedroom*

A Thatched Cottage and Addition in Wiltshire

This white painted, half-timbered and thatched cottage belonging to Professor and Mrs Guyatt in Wiltshire was originally very small, but they have added on a thatched and weather-boarded second half with great sympathy, joining the two together with a flat-roofed corridor.

The second half is really just one large studio room with a sleeping gallery and the Guyatt's have taken advantage of the high-pitched roof to make an interesting ceiling treatment inside, with tongue-and-grooved boarding supported by an axis that looks like the sturdy spokes of a wheel. The floor is quarry tiled and a slender spiral staircase leads up to the gallery. Floor to ceiling windows between the bookshelves lead out on to a new terrace, and the upper windows are made more interesting with a moulded arch, repeated in the door leading to the garden from the linking corridor.

The old part contains kitchen, dining room, workroom, bathroom, bedrooms and main hall with a new staircase going up at a more comfortable angle than the old boxed-in original. It is furnished with a casual mixture of country antiques and the occasional modern chair, and though very different in materials, the two halves of the cottage share remarkably much the same feeling, helped greatly by the consistent use of white throughout.

Above: *Hall*
Right: *Dining room*

Left: *A detail of the ceiling in the new extension* (below)

A Flint Cottage in Suffolk

Terence and Caroline Conran transformed their small labourer's cottage, built of Suffolk flint, into an easy casual series of rooms that lead one from another, so that everything and everybody are within easy reach. Nothing is complicated. From the pictures, it is easy to see that the interior has been radically altered from the original, but the outside, with the exception of the windows, has been left much as before.

You walk from gum-booted lobby into kitchen, through louvred doors into living room, from living room to bedroom, bathroom and staircase and other bedrooms upstairs. Rooms are punctuated by casual still-lives: a great bowl of nuts on the quarry tile floor; a long wooden table with a lily plant curling around an Edwardian pair of scales; a wicker fly swatter of unnatural size leaning against a bare white wall.

Sitting area and main bedroom are separated by a central chimney with a central fire, so that you can go to bed in the light of the dying flames and the scent of woodsmoke. But the two areas are equally divided by the difference in flooring: quarry tiles on the one side, stripped wood on the other. Plaster between the beams has been scooped away, the brickwork has been whitened, and walls are either white or tongue-and-grooved.

The kitchen is enviable. It is very much a cooking-eating room; sturdy, unpretentious, with tiled floor and tongue-and-grooved pine ceiling. Baskets of vegetables on the floor, stone jars, terra cotta bread troughs, shelves of comestibles, are all ingredients to whet the appetite.

Really the cottage is an object lesson in the unpretentious; a subtle example of the truly rural, with its exaggeration of natural assets, its quiet backgrounds.

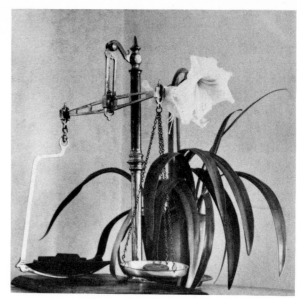

Below: *Kitchen and eating area*

Left: *Bedroom details*
Below: *Living room*

A Stone Farmhouse in Somerset

Lt. General Sir Brian and Lady Horrocks have achieved a most unmilitary triumph with their ancient stone farmhouse. It was a complete ruin when they first found it: impractical, crumbling and uncomfortable. But it was set in lovely rural unspoilt country, miles from noise and dirt and urban confusion, and with precise planning they have transformed it into a practical and beautiful home. Walls have been cut away, new ones built, the front entrance has been changed, the staircase has been opened up, natural details have been made much of, and the whole has been pleasantly and gently decorated.

Lady Horrocks has a subtle painter's eye, an idiosyncratic taste, a useful knowledge of when to stop. On the whole, all the ground floor rooms are tiled, and white walled, and the floors are either left bare, or covered here and there with oriental and rush mats. Upstairs, there is the same sparseness of detail. That is to say the natural detail of the house has been left to speak for itself, untrammelled by extraneous decoration.

The fireplace wall in the sitting room which is of unplastered stone has been whitewashed, and the deep window embrasures have been left uncurtained. A long squashy sofa is casually covered in a white and beige and tobacco tweed with cushions of yellow and orange and in this muted setting the dark woods of the furniture take on an added depth. Dining room and kitchen are furnished very similarly: the same quarry tiled floor in deep russets;

a long refectory table in each; a couple of dressers: one in pine for the kitchen, one in oak for the dining room. The dining room is grander with a deep stone fireplace; the kitchen is good plain homely fare with battered walls, impregnated with the smell of fresh herbs.

It is a very rural house, and it makes one particularly aware of the subtleties of natural textures and of restraint.

Left: *Kitchen*
Below: *Dining room*

42

Above: *Sitting room*
Right: *Sir Brian Horrocks' bedroom*
(with early Ambrose Heal bed)

A Gamekeeper's Cottage in East Anglia

When not in London, Angus Wilson has secreted himself for some years now, in this old gamekeeper's cottage in an East Anglian wood. The long, low flint walls are studded with roses, a belt of old shrub roses surrounds the house and these in turn give way to a thicket of trees. It is a writer's, anyone's, idyll.

Inside, rooms are small and spare but comfortable. Endless books are stacked on shelves juxtaposed with Victoriana, memorabilia, paintings of cats, stuffed birds in glass cases, and there is a general, casual clutter. Beams are whitened, floors are bricked and there is a pleasing mixture of periods. A Gothic chair for example, stands by an early nineteenth century painted corner cupboard grouped with a piece of multiple kinetic sculpture.

Structurally, very little has been done, at least in the way of altering walls and room sizes. But the house has been tended carefully, the garden has burgeoned with skilful planting. It is unmitigatedly English.

Three views of the living room

A Farm Cottage in Suffolk

This seventeenth century East Anglian cottage with its pink washed walls and tiled roof is an interesting example of completely cosmetic decoration, or disguise, achieved mostly with paint and wallpaper. Because it was only rented on a comparatively short lease, the occupants were uncertain of their or the cottage's future and loath to spend more of their money than was strictly necessary on making the interior presentable. But it badly needed rehabilitating, so much so that there had been talk in the village of bulldozing it down.

Although the position was enough to soften the most urban of hearts, set as it was half a mile up a long cart track, surrounded by sloping meadows and orchards, with the church in the distance, cows gently cropping the buttercups and a couple of ponds waiting to be cleared, the cottage itself seemed to be crumbling on its foundations. The lean-to was used as a chicken-cum-bicycle-and-tool shed, the tiny sitting room sported a new brick fireplace of some vulgarity as well as three different kinds of peeling wallpaper, two of the three bedrooms had holes in the floor and the front was almost hidden by a rotting, decrepit verandah. Windows were all broken, and the cloakroom next to the miniscule bathroom had no window or indeed ventilation of any sort.

The first steps were to pull down the verandah which meant letting in a surprising amount of new light; to clear away the lean-to of all extraneous chicken runs, guinea-pig cages, rabbit and stoat hutches and the carpenter's bench, to repair the windows, and dismantle the wall between bathroom and cloakroom which, in one stroke, made the bathroom bigger and got rid of an insanitary hole. This done, surprisingly inexpensively, all the more cracked and crumbling walls were held together with wallpaper, the lean-to was damp-proofed and whitewashed, the kitchen-living room was painted a warm orange, the hall and landing a deep maize, and the sitting room dark olive green with white beams. The offending fireplace was disguised as much as it could be with white paint, and the upstairs wallpapers were chosen for their variations on the oranges, yellows and greens downstairs. All the downstairs floors and the stairs and landing were covered with the cheapest possible sisal matting, and the tiny bedrooms were carpeted with off-cuts from an obliging carpet factory. The effect was suddenly of a space which bore no real relation to the actual measurements but was immediately gratifying.

Blinds were used at the windows instead of curtains, the furniture was a mixture of modern papier mâché, Habitat, junk shop finds and country antiques, and the entire furnishing and decorating bill came to less than £1,000.

Above: *Dining area of kitchen*
Right: *Bedroom views*

Right: *Children's bedroom*
Below: *Sitting room*

Eighteenth Century Brick and Tile in Buckinghamshire

Paul Anstee is a fastidious, harmonious and delicate decorator whose work is often spiced with a kind of ironic self-parody. His cottage in Buckinghamshire is neat, unassuming, set in a garden of great splendour that is full of healthily burgeoning delights and undulating, rural views. In fact the cottage was really bought for the prospect of its garden, the prospect itself, and the fact that it was a very easy drive from London.

The rooms were all tiny, but Mr Anstee left well alone and contented himself with decorating them as well as he could, satisfied with the major delight to him, of the garden outside. He likes cooking, so his kitchen is stuffed with herbs and cooking apparatus and workmanlike benches and tables where he entertains his friends. He likes talking and his sitting room is relaxed and cluttered and comfortable and full of greenery and flowers. He likes comfort particularly, and his two bedrooms are pretty and warm and bucolic in a mildly urban way. But the *pièce de résistance* is his bathroom (which also acts as flower room), and is lined with bark, and ceiling'd with trellis, and appears covered in flowers and greenery.

Right: *Sitting room*
Below left: *Kitchen*
Below centre: *Bedroom*
Below right: *Bathroom/Flower room*

54

Conversions

What constitutes a conversion? For my purposes, or the purposes of this chapter, it is the repair, building-up, the turning into a reasonable home of any building which was either not a dwelling place in the first instance, or else not fit to live in, at least in the style envisaged, at the time of purchase. It does not, in this instance, include illustrations of rehabilitated cottages and farmhouses, although all the rules that I outline here apply to them, because I have already dealt with them in the previous chapter.

Since the desire for a second house is as much therapeutic as anything else, it follows that a number of people find the therapy starts with the exercise of turning the impractical, the unobvious, into the practical and desirable. A building that was not at first intended as a house often has the asset of unusual space, or unusual height, and almost invariably, of excellent position. In any event, it is always something of a triumph to turn the unpromising into the civilized.

Conversion is sometimes almost as expensive as building from scratch. Occasionally more so. But it does have the advantage to the amateur, or the uninitiated, that ready-made clothes have over custom-built ones. At least you can envisage what you are getting. Or the site may be particularly good. Or the building and its site may be very cheap. And the chief advantage of all, though it often escapes the notice of those who have not battled with local authorities before, is the fact that it is usually very much easier to get

'. . . it is best to leave the original structure of any old building as undisturbed as possible . . .'

planning permission to alter and enlarge an existing building, than it is for starting afresh.

Europe and the British Isles are so blessed with their numbers of ancient buildings lying empty, neglected and forlorn in their tangled but enviable settings that it seems a disgrace not to nurture them more carefully. Besides, more often than not, you can get improvement grants for old buildings from your local council of up to £1,000 or half the cost of the work, whichever is less. And should your building be of historical value and listed as such, you should qualify for an additional grant from your local authority to put special features in order, though you may find you are limited in what you may do to its external and sometimes its internal appearance.

The great point to remember when applying for a grant is that no work *to be covered by the grant*

can be started until you have made a written application to the council and have back from them their approval in writing. It is important that your application should be backed by detailed estimates of the cost of the proposed work from at least two builders and by Planning and Building Regulation approval. The council will want to be satisfied that the planning alterations satisfy regulations, and reassured that the price is tolerably competitive, although they will not necessarily make you accept the cheapest estimate. It is in their interest, too, that the work is well done.

All this may well take several months, and if time means money to you, it might well be cheaper not to apply for a grant at all, particularly as for some reason best known to bureaucracy, you have to apply to apply. But if time is not of paramount importance then it is certainly worth while to contact the local council offices or town hall in order to find out more about the Improvement and Standard Grants to which you might be entitled. You can also buy a Ministry of Housing booklet called 'Money to Modernize your Home' which sets out everything in helpful detail.

The physical act of converting an old building requires a good deal of application. It does no harm to read about or study the features of as many similar buildings as possible; the sort of roof or roofing materials most commonly used and to make a note of indigenous building materials to that area. The worst thing you could do is to apply alien details that are inconsistent with the structure. Even if you decide to employ an architect in the conversion (and any work that is likely to cost over £1,000 well merits some architectural help), it is as well that you too have an eye, and a sensitive eye, to detail. It is remarkable how many architects, particularly members of rural firms, are deficient on that point.

An architect of course is almost indispensable for any building with specific problems, like a school or chapel. He should be able to work out whether you can insert a second floor into an old classroom, for example—and this can often be helped by excavating the floor underneath—or whether it would be best to take advantage of the soaring space and merely build a sleeping or study gallery instead. He can advise you on what walls you must leave untramelled because they are load-bearing, and what walls you can dispense with because they were simply partitions; where you can alter or build on, and where you cannot.

In principle, it is best to leave the original structure of any old building as undisturbed as possible and to add separate rooms if you need more space. One particularly successful converter of a sixteenth century barn added on two inconspicuous wings behind the main structure to form three sides of a square with a swimming pool in the middle, and the barn itself is left as a great transcending space with a sleeping gallery at one end, a music room gallery at the other.

The architect can also save you a great deal of tedium by dealing with all the boring things like suggesting suitable heating schemes, finding out legal snags to proposed alterations, dealing with the Local Authority, obtaining planning permission for any alterations that need permission, applying for any of the grants that you may be entitled to, estimating how much the structure will cost to run and maintain, finding and supervising a builder and generally co-ordinating the whole operation. Moreover the total cost of the whole, including his fees, *could* be considerably less than you would have had to pay if you had carried out your own ideas without his help, if only because it is difficult for the layman, however ingenious, to think in the necessary three-dimensional terms.

If you feel that the job really is not big enough for an architect, or are particularly shy of using one, there is an acceptable alternative in using a Chartered Surveyor. Big firms have their own drawing office with a resident architect and they can make your life considerably easier, once you have discussed with them what you want, by drawing up plans and specifications, preparing details of joinery work, handling all the paperwork and conscientiously seeing a job through. Smaller firms will undertake the same spade work, with the exception that without an architect's department you could not expect them to be quite so full of ideas on the planning side, so that much of the onus will be on you. This

can be advantageous if you are very inventive yourself, but lack the technical knowledge to put your plans on paper, for they will always look after that side of things, and you will still feel entirely responsible for the aesthetics. The charges are the same as an architect's.

If your financial situation, or your independence of mind, puts an architect's or surveyor's services beyond the pale and you have a big conversion job on hand you will need to be self-disciplined. Think long and hard before you start. What are the maximum number of rooms that you will need? Can these be found from existing space, or will additional building be required? Can you use roof or attic space, or if not now, later when you feel more financially viable? Think well ahead. Reflect very earnestly before rejecting the idea of installing heating at this stage. Even if you only intend to use it as a summer house now, you might well want to use it all the year round later, and it will cost a great deal more to put in in the future.

Think very carefully about lighting. Not just the position of plugs and switches and how many of each, but *how* you want each room to be lit. If you are lowering ceilings, for example, you can install inconspicuous recessed spots much more cheaply than at any time in the future—and spots and uplighters are a particularly subtle way to light old walls. You can put in rheostats or dimmers in a way that you could never afterwards achieve without a good deal of confusion.

It is important to put down on paper, in great detail, every single job that has to be tackled in the house. It should be so concise, so decisive, that the builder has no need to ask for explanations, take decisions, or have any leeway whatsoever for misunderstanding in the matter of cost. It should include all the work that your original survey advised you to have carried out; anything the mortgage company (if you are dealing with one) insists on as a condition to the loan; any work you must carry out to qualify for a grant; any work required by the Public Health department, District Surveyor and Borough Engineer, and any additional work you have thought of yourself.

When you are sure that you have written down absolutely everything that should be done, it is advisable to divide up the work into what needs doing on the exterior, and what should be done on the interior, room by room and floor by floor. Put the plumbing and electrical works under separate headings. And above all remember to visualize each room in its entirety, which means taking in everything from skirting boards to door furniture. State, for instance, exactly how many coats of paint you want, specifying that cracks should be filled and old flaky paint burnt off. Name the makes of the appliances you want fitted, and say exactly where and how you want them fixed. State what pipes you want to be concealed or boxed-in; what you want put in place of things you have asked to be removed. The list is enormous. So

think carefully and exhaustively.

It might be taxing at the time but the amount of money it will save in the long run is immense. Although it is not strictly necessary, particularly if your house is to be rather informal, it often helps to avoid confusion, recrimination and deep depression when you get your final bill, if you prepare a scheme of decoration to send in with your specification. Otherwise you will find builders allowing provisional sums for the decoration of rooms which can be very misleading to the amateur converter, as their idea of what you will choose for a room may be quite wrong. In any case you will have to present the builder you finally choose with a clearly-written scheme of decoration at some stage if you want to avoid costly and sometimes irreparable mistakes. If, when he has the (preferably typed) scheme in his possession, he still makes a mistake, all you have to do is wave your carbon copy at him and he is forced to make good at his own expense.

Give the builder the list, preferably with samples of papers, if any, and colours attached. Keep a copy of it yourself, and, if possible pin up a copy of the appropriate sheet on the wall of each room as well, so that the painters or wall-paper-hangers can refer to them if the foreman is not around. This way you should be able to avoid trouble even though you are having a building converted miles away from your home, making it impossible to make site visits as often as you would like.

However carefully you prepare your specification, it is almost inevitable that extras will crop up, so it is advisible in an ideal world, to try to keep a sum firmly in reserve for emergencies. In an old building, disturbances by work in progress might reveal all sorts of unsuspected faults, quite reasonably not discovered by the surveyor. In a building so ruined and dilapidated that you thought it of little use to hire a surveyor except for depression's sake, you will obviously just have to feel your way, and here it is all the more important to keep an emergency float.

Try to visit the house yourself as often as possible, to check that work is progressing and to iron out any problems. Keep notes of every point you will want to raise with the builder as they occur to you. You can forget them very easily if you do not take this simple precaution.

As for finding the right builder, this is really such a question of luck in an area you do not know and where you might not have friends to guide you. You could always ask the local authority who should be able to give you a list of names, and from there you should try to discover which builder is the best equipped for your particular job. If your building is of stone and crumbling you will need someone with a good mason. If there is a lot of joinery you will need an expert carpenter, and so on. You should always try to get two to three estimates to be compared, and here your careful specification, duplicated for each firm, should come into its own.

Examine their estimates in detail. Are they all specifying a good quality paint for the outside walls if needs be, and the same number of coats? (This is an instance where a clear direction on your specification will save much time and trouble). Are you sure they are all estimating for the same amount of work and materials? Compare all their provisional costs. Note where there are fixed prices and where there are fluctuating prices. Are there any conditions in small print on the back of the estimate which should be read over thoroughly? Denials of obligation, for example, if workmen cause damage by breakage or fire; loopholes to enable the builder to wriggle out of all sorts of complications.

Resist the temptation to immediately choose the cheapest price (unless you have heard particularly good things about the firm; and some builders charge less because they are better organised), since the low sum might betray a builder more concerned to land a contract than to carry out satisfactory work. If the final sums quoted only vary minutely, then be guided by factors like which firm gives the earliest firm finishing date; which is the largest (large firms have less to sub-contract), and the sort of foreman the firm promises to put on the job.

No conversion is easy. A conversion of any scale, without an architect or surveyor to oversee it, is less easy still. And a conversion tucked miles away in the country without easy access, is hardest of all. You will have to rely very heavily on your builder, unless you are going to spend patient months, perhaps years, doing it yourselves with the aid of the occasional odd job men. So it is important to establish rapport and keep a firm check.

The conversions I have shown here, ranging from a windmill to a railway station, vary greatly in style and execution, but they all share the preservationists crusading spirit to rehabilitate the decrepit; to make the best of a building on a beautiful site.

A Medieval Barn Complex in Sussex

Conversion is hardly an adequate word for the aggregate of time, care, sensitivity and subtlety spent by Miss Fleur Cowles and her husband on the transformation of this magnificent tithe barn. The swimming pool behind it had been in existence for some years, but it was only recently that they started to work on making the ancient structure that had hitherto done service as a car shelter, into comfortable—even exotic—living space.

The whole building was virtually dismantled: tiles and beams were carefully annotated, and reassembled complete with appropriate but concealed lagging, plumbing, insulation, heating; and then a sliding glass wall looking over the pool area, windows, and two extensions were added at the back, so that the pool is enclosed on three sides. Now the complete complex—which from the front elevation looks scarcely changed, includes a huge living area with a gallery at either end (one of them for music), plus, in one extension, a kitchen, cloakroom, shower room, a sauna, and two changing rooms, all simply brick-walled and quarry tile-floored. And in the other, a double bedroom and bathroom.

Plaster between the beams in the main area is painted with the palest grey-blue wash, whilst shelves, the tables encircling the support beams, and the stairs going up to the music gallery, are a dark, glossy rich claret. Vivid colours flicker against the calm background: apple red lamp shades, the gamut of fuchsia pinks and oranges; woven and bril-liant patchwork tablecloths, splendid cushions and rugs and memorabilia, and paintings of course, and piles of books. There is a long brown suede chesterfield, a lot of early Brazilian furniture, fresh red and white cotton cushion covers on purple and white cotton covered banquettes. And then there are particular Cowles touches like the stuffed owl in the bookcase standing in front of her owl triptych with its orange flame background; the *faux* Zebra skin, the antiquities and modern playthings tucked in among the books.

Miss Cowles idiosyncratic decoration, her sure sense of colour and juxtaposition, is certainly not in the English tradition, but then it is not in the American tradition either. It is a distillation rather, of her great travels, her interests, her friends, her arts, but a very twentieth century distillation at that.

Photograph by Norman Parkinson
(By kind permission of Condé Nast)

Three views of the main living area

A Ruined Essex Coach House Revived

Seven or eight years ago this Gothic coach house called 'The Ring' was a complete wreck lying dormant and neglected in the verdant tangle of woods surrounding Audley End in Essex. Miss Elizabeth Hanley came across it quite by accident one wet Sunday, fell in love with it, arranged for its lease to be handed to her, and has been resuscitating house and garden ever since.

It was originally built in 1776 by the fourth Lord Howard de Walden, though it is thought that some kind of structure existed there before, and there is a legend that Charles II used to meet Nell Gwyn on that very spot. Certainly there is a plantation near by called the Charles Plantation. Anyway, it is all very romantic. Undeterred, indeed, inspired, Miss Hanley has treated the decoration of the house with great subtlety. It is gentle, languorously faded, the detailing so subtle, the colours so muted, the garden so bucolic with roses rampaging through the trees; an avenue of apple trees marching up the lawn; an old cart propped negligently in a corner; that one wants to visit it again and again. And then there is the prevailing smell of woodsmoke that surrounds the house with a special aura, and of course, the woods themselves, cradling the house and garden; quietly restrained, but only just.

The outside is a mixture of eighteenth century Gothic and nineteenth century barge-boarding, with arches and mouldings repeating themselves through various aspects of the building. For example, the flagged hall with its *trompe l'œil* panelling and *faux marbre* opens out to the garden on one side through a series of three arches, and these arches are repeated in turn in the bookcases in the sitting room which opens off the hall at right angles. Even the Gazebo at the end of the garden is Gothicized and emulates one of John Fowler's, the English decorator *par excellence,* and obviously a great inspiration to Miss Hanley.

Since Miss Hanley believes that the weekends are for entertaining, the house is particularly arranged for that purpose. The kitchen, which is the real centre of the house, is full of scrubbed pine and copper, with a Colefax-Fowler trellis print at the windows in blue-and-white. The hall also acts as dining room with a central round table with a floor length ultramarine blue cloth, and this, together with the sitting room with its fawns and pinks and comfortable country house colours, makes a particularly good party space. Upstairs there are two double bedrooms and a single room, and there is also a downstairs garden room-spare room with its own bathroom. All are prettily chintzed, comfortably bedded, gently idiosyncratic.

In its earlier days, the house was clearly 'a cottage of gentility' geared for the gentry's idea of the simple life, with the servants nicely tucked away in the background. It is extraordinary that no one thought to rescue it before.

Far left: *Gazebo*
Left: *Garden elevation*
Below: *Sitting room*

Above: *Dining room/hall*
Right: *Two bedrooms*

An Oast House on the Sussex-Kent Borders

Oast houses have always been good subjects for conversion and this one on the Sussex-Kent borders is an admirable example. Mr. Geoffrey Sharpe the restaurateur who has done much to convert our taste in food, has been equally successful with this project. When he and his partner, Mr John Schlesinger, the film director, first discovered it, it was a peculiarly inconvenient structure in an idyllically rural setting. It was derelict, rotting, disorganized. With the help of David Hicks, they have managed to turn it into a practical, spacious and comfortable weekend house. The garden slopes away to a stream which borders the edge of their land, the view burgeons with trees in full maturity, and the interplay of spaces within the house should please any student of architecture.

Basically, the structure consists of two houses joined by the house proper which is handsomely weather-boarded in the idiom of the area. You now walk through the front door into an airy, *provençal*-tiled hall, which in turn opens out into a long kitchen and round tented sitting room in one of the oast houses. The other oast house provides a large, fabric-lined fresh green and white bedroom on the ground floor with a centrally placed and canopied bed, and both have two more bedrooms on top. Above the hall, which is also used for eating (there are two different sized tables for differing parties, differing occasions), there is a large, double-height studio-living room, and yet more bedrooms and bathrooms. This floor

is reached by an interesting, clean-cut staircase in steel and wood designed by David Hicks.

The detailing throughout the house is of particular interest, not just in the arrangement of objects, but in the juxtaposition of furniture, fabrics and colours. The two main bedrooms in the round oast house rooms have been beautifully handled. The one all deep blue and white with a Gothicised screen for a wardrobe, the other brown and red with a centrally placed and canopied bed as on the ground floor. Another bedroom is all white and looks memorably chaste and innocent, and a bathroom with its brown paper walls edged and pannelled with a tobacco and red border, the bath curtained with tweed, is extremely handsome.

The conversion is a classic exercise in comfort, decoration and space.

Below: *Two exterior views and new staircase*
Right: *New living room*
Below right: *Dining area*

Above left: *Another dining area*
Above right: *Detail of living room ceiling*
Centre, below and left: *Details of bedrooms*

Above: *Bedroom detail*
Right: *Bathroom*
Below right and opposite: *Two guest rooms*

A Windmill and Granary in Sussex

Mr Henry Longhurst, the golfer and writer, and his wife, live in, and between, two well-known Sussex landmarks, known as the Jack and Jill Windmills. One has been left unconverted, the other houses Mr Longhurst's study-workroom and what appears to be a series of spiralling chapels, or rooms for meditation, or just plain studios. Anyway, they are lovely, inaccessible (except to the nimble) rooms which have to be clambered-up to. They can afford to be follies, for the main living space and more conventional living rooms and bedrooms are housed in a modern building in between the two mills, cleverly designed and weather-boarded so that it has become an integral part of the complex.

Although they seem to be attractive prospects for conversion, windmills are very seldom practical. They are usually too tall, and because of their necessary angle, any stairway is usually too precipitous for comfort. Round room succeeds round room in seemingly endless layers, but by mostly living in the space between the mills and granary, and using the mills themselves for quiet and work, or parties and other extra-mural activities, the Longhursts have made the best of both worlds. And their views over the Sussex downs from all angles are quite extraordinary.

Above: *Chapel room*
Right: *Exterior of one of the windmills*
Far right: *Study*

An Abandoned Northumbrian Railway Station

Old railway stations long since disused, their gauges grassed over, their signal boxes tangled with vines, are a natural subject for conversion. In one complex there are waiting rooms, booking offices, signal boxes, and very often the station master's quarters as well, all waiting to be turned into comfortable living space. The platform can form a terrace, the line itself a sunken lawn, and bridges are always a highly decorative adjunct to a garden.

This sturdy stone station in Northumberland, only a few miles from Hadrian's Wall, had the particular advantage of being perched above a river so that it overlooked two bridges crossing railway and water. Now the old sleepers have been removed and the line runs in a green curve of turf underneath a bridge dripping with roses to the extreme comfort of swimming pool and Sauna bath.

The owners and converters, Mr and Mrs Fewster, have preserved many of the old ingredients: the lamps, the ticket desk and counter (which makes a useful alcove for the display of various objects), the old labelling, and in the hall, the station master's bell, his oil lamp, and a framed First Class Award for being the Best Kept Station some decades back. Grouped together it makes a touching still life and a constant reminder, should one be needed, of the origins of their now very comfortable house with its plethora of modern conveniences.

Three views of the station exterior

Comfortable Country

There are few nations with as many small country houses as the British Isles. They cluster comfortably in between the definitions of mansions on the one hand and cottages on the other, but to many they are the epitome of British or Irish rural life. They are the Manor Houses and Halls, Granges and Places, Priories and Pavilions, Vicarages and Rectories, large Farmhouses and Mill Houses, and they are scattered over every county in a liberal profusion.

They conjure up lovely visions of mellow'd brickwork or creeper'd plaster set in a multi-green frame of oak and beech, mulberry and walnut, chestnut and elm and the occasional cedar. Surrounded by lawns and shrubberies, herbaceous borders and rose gardens, they repose dreamily in the sweet-smelling air, absorbing the sounds of birds and bees, the buzz of lawn mowers and the click and muttered imprecations of croquet. Leisurely tennis is played on velvety grass, lunch is on the terrace, tea is under the trees, 'And oft between the boughs is seen the sly shade of a rural dean.' For us, as for Rupert Brooke, these visions are almost always set in a perpetual flaming June. Though even in winter, with the sharp clean smell of frost, the spanking golden air, the crackling leaves underfoot, the curling fragrant woodsmoke out, and the blazing fires within, the idyllic vision is scarcely diminished.

Charming, evocative, idiosyncratic and peaceful as they all may be, they are not, alas, always comfortable. Indeed, the charm, evoca-

'. . . charming, evocative, idiosyncratic and peaceful . . .'

tion, idiosyncracy, peace and loveliness is often totally undermined by this lack. Notorious British draughts whistle under the graceful doors and through the cracks in the picturesque battered plaster. The famous blazing log fires do little to alleviate the still damp cold stored up through unheated centuries. Bathrooms are not always so much in evidence, or so near to bedrooms, as they would be in a more ideal world. Damp seeps up walls innocent of damp-proof courses, and the electricity supply in the country is far from reliable.

I know one ancient tawny stone house in the Cotswolds, whose roses tendril up the walls and in through the deep window embrasures; whose lawns lie green and velvet in the shade of great, voluptuous oaks; and whose kitchen smells perpetually of freshly baking bread. The food is imaginative and the drink prolific and it is forever England.

But as soon as Autumn comes one is presented at the door with a ritual blanket and a large silk handkerchief. The blanket to sit huddled in as a warder-off of draughts or to wrap round as extra cover for hurried forays down freezing corridors. The handkerchief to wipe away the slobber of the over-emotional dogs.

At least the owners recognize the shortcomings of the house and try to provide some sort of antidote however cosmetic, however ironic. But for many a permanent country-dweller, oblivious, through long exposure, to the shortcomings of his house, the chief virtue in his guests is toughness. For, for some reason, a large proportion of the British think it not only more admirable to suffer the cold and wide-flung windows in silence, but are convinced that central heating is not only molly-coddling but positively unhealthy.

In the event, the part-time country dweller is more pampered. For if he is determined to buy a small country house complete with trappings, he is likely, too, to want the best of both worlds, his rurality spiced with comfort however, inconspicuous and discreet. And simply because the house is at least temporarily an escape rather than a full-time home, a civilized, idealistic and tolerably affluent owner is likely to try to make the house as near as he can an escapist's paradise.

Moreover, it is a curious fact that whilst people are prepared to camp in a cottage, or a small farmhouse, or even a castle, for the sake of the ambience, or the view, or the peace and solitude, they are inclined to expect something more from a country house *per se*. They want their enjoyment of the country untrammelled by indifferent plumbing, heating and lack of normal amenities. In short, for their pleasure to be perfect, they want their country houses to be comfortable.

Real, deep comfort is not necessarily synonymous with original design or decoration. It is more a question of warmth, both physical and mental; of easeful bedrooms and living rooms; of prettiness; of well-arranged flowers, objects, paintings. It is also a sense of detail and colour and of maximizing natural ingredients to show to their best advantage, and above all it is a general air of welcome and well-being. It is a difficult quality to achieve with subtlety, because one wants to be conscious of it, rather than assailed by it; eased and calmed rather than suffocated. And comfort has to be as easy on the eye, as on the body, as on the mind. When a house achieves all these things, then it is truly a place to be looked back on with nostalgia.

An Old Rectory in County Donegal

Mr Rory Cameron always makes beautiful houses, and his properties in France have been, and are, outstanding. This little house in Ireland where he spends a month here and there throughout the year, was a former rectory, built in the eighteenth century, and of an extreme simplicity. Inside it is very pretty, with a mixture of rare early American furniture, as well as English and Irish pieces. Colours are subtle: ivories and buffs, clear cool greys and white, with the occasional William Morris wallpaper and fresh chintz.

He has used simple matting to particular effect in the dining room, and his bathrooms, too, are good, with the blue and white tiling and chintz in the one, the chinoiserie in the other. The drawing room is all gentle parchment colour and white with the sudden juxtaposition of a fierce Kenneth Noland painting, and the library has some particularly splendid furniture. In fact the contrast of the interior with its quiet, comfortable sophistication, and the severe homespun exterior set haphazardly among the long grass and the trees, is a good Irish contradiction, well in the Celtic tradition.

Above: *Library*
Below: *The drawing room*

84

Above: *Bedroom*
Above right: *The dining room*
Below right: *Another bedroom*

Above left: *Study*
Below left and below: *Two bath-rooms*

A Sixteenth Century Farmhouse

Most people, one supposes, would think Miss Fleur Cowles' house the epitome of comfortable country living. A large sixteenth century farmhouse set in the middle of steeply dipping wooded meadows. The house itself, irregularly tiled and half timbered with brick nogging scarcely discernible through the vines, roses and creepers, set against great trees in full foliage, and well-shrubbed lawns unfurling down to the stream below. The interior: warm and cool in season, permeated with the sweet, lingering smell of woodsmoke, full of paintings, and idiosyncrasy and warm colour, and of course people. One must not forget the people. It all seems too good to be true. But it is true, and much treasured as such, by Miss Cowles and her husband.

Walking in through a well-planted porch and inner hall, you come immediately into a long sweep of room, with a herringbone brick floor, massive fireplace, comfortable sofas, and two dining tables. The tables are always covered in frivolously flowered floor length tablecloths; the china is *provençal* or South American, or Spanish, or Italian depending on the dish or the mood; the dining chair seats are covered in pink and white gingham, and other odd tables: round tables, long tables, side tables, are loaded with every sort of eclectic find, a great collection of false food and fruit, ceramic chickens, bowls of flowers.

The siting room is just as idiosyncratic. Walls and ceiling are painted a dark brown between the beams. Wide oak plank floors are partially covered with rug. Two comfortable armchairs and a sofa are covered in red, another sofa in brown and white *toile de Jouy*. Windows are pelmeted with *gros point* in red and green, and tables are massed with books; walls with paintings.

Upstairs, the bedrooms are entirely individual, filled with the sort of memorabilia that only a lifetime of inveterate travelling and collecting can provide. Miss Cowles' own bedroom has a wall of windows from floor to ceiling opposite the bed, to take maximum advantage of the changing seasons outside. The bed is covered in a handsome patchwork quilt, the polished boards are scattered with woven rugs, and a stark little desk and tomato-covered chair are silhouetted against the light. Another bedroom is totally red with a dark blue and red bedcover and tester. A third is pale blue in between the beams, with a lace-covered four poster and scarlet night lights; a fourth, beamed and pink and white. And a fifth attic bedroom cum sitting room, has matching tomato and white chintz in between the beams on the sloping ceiling, and on the sofa and chairs, with a small skirted table in red felt, topped with fresh white lace like a pristine altar boy's cotter.

89

Above left: *Recumbent sculpture in the garden*
Above right: *Corner of the dining room*
Above: *View of the main bedroom*
Right: *The sitting room*

Below: *Detail from the hall*
Four bedrooms

A Manor House in Wiltshire

When Mr David and Lady Mary Russell first found Coombe Manor in Wiltshire it was in a sorry state of disrepair, having been totally neglected for the past 25 years. The present drawing room was shut up, the kitchen was at best primitive, water was coming in through the upstairs rooms, and there was virtually no heating. The builders were in the house a year before the family could move in, practically re-roofing the house, re-wiring, putting in central heating and generally restoring, though the only actual structural changes that the Russells made were to pull down a wall half way across what is now the enormous drawing room, and to change the position of the front door. Even now some two or three years later, they claim that the house is only half finished. But that half is really the epitome of the Englishness of English style.

Although the front elevation of the house is mellow William and Mary, it was originally the site of an old monastery. In the sixteenth century, a modest Elizabethan farmhouse was built with three gables; and the staircase and some of the old rafters in the roof space still remain as relics. Finally, the William and Mary house was built around the lot, and another storey was added to counteract the slope of the site. Now it sits comfortably tucked down in a fold in the hills with its quiet garden and lovely out-house groupings stretching away behind it. At one end of the walled garden there is a gazebo, still waiting for restoration, and there are all the yards and courtyards and terraces and barns that make for perfect childhood play.

Inside, the hall is large and light and airy, with delicate cornices and pilasters, a good fireplace, white pannelling and a pretty arched entrance to inner hall and staircase. There are some fine pieces of eighteenth and early nineteenth century furniture, books, magazines, flowers, a handsome chinz at the windows in deep pink and moss greens and the whole is based on a tough, practical haircord carpet.

The large drawing room is a particularly good example of the grand *Style Anglaise*. It has white panelling, chaste cornices, long, graceful, shuttered windows, two splendid fireplaces, a fine gilt and marble-topped side table, mirrors, paintings, books, and a great many comfortable armchairs and sofas. All one would hope to find, in short, in the classic English drawing room.

The main bedroom is also very handsome with its four poster bed curtained and covered with chintz and lace, and lined with shirred pink. Walls are pale pink framed with a thin line of red, and carpet and wainscoting are white.

But the great triumph of the house is the kitchen. Mostly lined in pine with large terracotta tiles underfoot, it has a series of good-looking pine cupboards, some of them topped, and others backed with blue and white ceramic tiles. Oven and hob are built-in, and there is a large comfortable refectory table for family eating.

Although many people might

consider Coombe Manor rather large for a weekend and holiday house, it must be remembered that the Russells are a large family. In any event, the house has been furnished and accoutred with such sensible moderation and such practicality that it has become a model of its kind.

Above: *The drawing room*
Right: *The kitchen*

Left: *The hall*
Below: *Main bedroom*

An East Anglian Mill House

Mill houses are almost always a comfortable, leisurely, unpretentious hotch-potch, and spatially interesting, too, if the mill buildings have been converted. Add to this the bonus of being surrounded by water, and mill houses will be seen to be among the most coveted of country houses.

The Stanhope Sheltons' millhouse in Suffolk, originally constructed by Sir Francis and Lady Meynoll is an enviable example. Mostly seventeenth century with an eighteenth century front, it rambles alongside, and over the river; a cluster of shapes and colours and textures, from Suffolk pink-washed brick and plaster to creosoted weather-boarding to glass (for the river-bridging room) to classic whitewashed boarding for the mill itself. And then there is the astonishing double height studio-gallery that Stanhope Shelton has made for himself, linking it to the main building by a covered walk.

The garden dips down into the water, judiciously placed willows dabble in the ripples, and statuary appears here and there, swathed in broad-leafed plants, rearing through the irises. It appears as perfect a setting as one can reasonably expect.

The studio with its monumental longitudinally slashed windows, is all white and cosy inside. Pale polished wood floors downstairs, hair cord carpeting in the gallery, and a massed collection of English water-colours and drawings and Mies Barcelona chairs.

The main house is much more eclectic. Floor levels change, as do architectural styles, and rooms meander one from another. Eighteenth century mouldings and arches give way to beams and low ceilings; eighteenth and nineteenth century drawings give way to twentieth century abstracts. Possessions, books, the memorabilia of enquiring minds are everywhere.

Above: *Detail of the mill pond*
Right: *Front elevation*
Below: *Studio*

Above: *Sitting room*
Right: *Another view of the studio*
Below: *Hall and dining room*

A Wiltshire Rectory

Rectories and vicarages, long since dispensed with by an indigent, or at least a prudent church, make some of the nicest possible country houses. This one, belonging to Sir Robin and Lady Darwin, is no exception. It is made up of an assembly of seventeenth century, Victorian and Edwardian parts, with Gothick touches subtly added by Sir Robin in the library and the Summer House. And in the attics, there is a great studio. One must not forget that. It is an indispensable part of the house.

The house stands high in one of those ideal Wiltshire villages which, undeterred by the twentieth century, consists only of one or two pleasant, largish houses, some unspoilt cottages and a village shop—or so it seemed to me. Built of soft red brick with a prodigious tangle of wistaria, it rises from level to level, from roof pitch to roof pitch, out of a pre-eminently English garden which sweeps and curves in a splendid stretch of turf and herbaceous borders to a coppice of trees, a tangle of long grass, and then a vista of meadows.

Inside it is beautifully furnished. The library is a classic of its kind with book-lined walls and an elaborate cornice; all ochres and browns and oriental rugs. The drawing room is pale and subtle: grey silk walls and grey carpet, pretty eighteenth century furniture, masses of flowers and unexpected paintings by Leonard Rosoman. The dining room is best-English, and upstairs, bedrooms are comfortable, even gay. Lady Darwin's study-boudoir

is all dark green walls and deep rose, with a white and rose *chaise-longe*. Her bedroom, united to the room next door by a pale grey carpet, has rose and grey wallpaper, a rose and anthracite Welsh bedspread, mixing pattern with pattern with easy success.

Just as the garden is geared for croquet (well, almost) so the house is geared for guests. It has become a renowned place for splendid English weekends.

Top left: *Corner of the drawing room*
Top centre: *Library*
Top right: *Sir Robin's studio*
Bottom: *Two bedrooms and the gothick garden room*

A Pair of Inigo Jones Pavilions in Northamptonshire

Mr Robin Chancellor had been looking for a house in the country —'a bolt-hole', as he said, for some time, when, nearly 20 years ago now, he saw an article in *Country Life* by Arthur Oswald, describing a pair of derelict seventeenth century pavilions, almost certainly executed by Inigo Jones, to designs brought to him from Italy by Sir Walter Crane, the successful director of the Mortlake Tapestry works. The pavilions were all that was left of Stoke Park, Stoke Bruerne, which was the first English country house to display the typical Palladian plan of a central block with balancing pavilions linked to it by colonnades or screen walls. Begun in about 1630 and finished before 1640, it was built, remarkably, some 80 years before Lord Burlington and his architects revived the cult of Palladio to become an almost standardised pattern of the eighteenth century.

In Victorian times the main building was destroyed by fire, and towards the end of the century was rebuilt on the lines of an Elizabethan manor house. This had been unoccupied since 1938. Happily the pavilions had been left but by that time they were in a pitiful state of disrepair, and Mr Oswald finished his article with a *cri de coeur*. 'As a . . . landmark in the evolution of the Renaissance architecture in this country, they would have high claims for preservation on that score alone. But as they were almost certainly designed by Inigo Jones, the claims should be undeniable.

Unfortunately their present state is such that unless active steps are taken in the near future, they will be past preserving.'

Mr Chancellor and his partner, Mr André Révai, were moved by this sad tale, and straightway went to inspect the pavilions. The colonnades were in ruins, the garden overgrown, the main house monstrous, but they bravely saw the possibilities for salvation. After a year of negotiations, they finally managed to buy the property, together with nine acres of land, and proceeded to demolish the Victorian mansion and recondition the pavilions, with the help of a generous grant allotted by the Historic Buildings Council in much the way suggested by Mr Marshall Sisson in his report for the Society for the Preservation of Ancient Buildings. That is to say by concentrating on turning the East pavilion (which already possessed drainage and services and thus the bones of a habitable house) into their main dwelling, and making the other one, which had originally been a huge library, into a garden room. It took them two years to restore the East pavilion, and the accommodation now consists of a large and beautiful drawing room and four bedrooms, with a kitchen and dining room in the basement. They used an old fire escape instead of a conventional staircase to the upper floor, and exaggerated the light and airiness of the drawing room by their subtle use of colour: pale grey-greens and dark duck egg blues, with a plain white dado, an off-white haircord carpet and Samarkand rugs. They had good pictures and a certain amount of handsome family furniture, and really for the rest, the rooms were so beautiful, the decoration virtually took care of itself.

It took another five years to get the garden into the sort of order they wanted, but the end result, the juxtaposition of water, stone and green, is very splendid. The pavilions must make the most elegant bolt-hole imaginable.

Opposite: *The drawing room*

Castles, Towers and Follies

Castles—originally built as private fortresses for the king and his nobles—have an assiduously romantic appeal in this century. Although it would be folly indeed for a private individual in this day and age to erect from scratch the sort of romantic Gothick follies put up in the eighteenth and nineteenth centuries, there are still people with fervour enough not only to live in Gothick castles, but to go to almost any lengths to restore and rehabilitate the more ancient ruins scattered so purposefully around the British Isles.

To understand their crusading spirit one should go back over the history of castle building in these countries, which in effect is not only the history of defence but of extraordinary technical, stoic and aesthetic achievement.

The first real fortress was introduced into England just before the Norman conquest by a knight called Richard Fitzcrob. He was in fact a Norman, one of the reinforcements invited over from France by Edward the Confessor to help defend the Welsh border, and he built himself a fortress near Ludlow in Shropshire, modelled on the kind currently being built in his native Normandy. That is to say it was made by digging a wide circular ditch and throwing the earth in the middle to form a mound. This mound, called a motte, was flattened on top and a strong wooden fence or palisade was erected round the summit. Inside this fence, in the space known as the bailey, a brightly painted wooden tower was built to

'... there are still people with fervour enough to live in Gothic castles ...'

serve as dwelling house and the last point of defence.

When Duke William of Normandy arrived himself in 1066 to become so precipitantly William the Conqueror of England, the first thing he did was to erect a timber and earth fortress at Hastings. After the battle, he then marched on to Dover and is said to have enlarged a similar castle built some time before by the unfortunate King Harold. All in all, he is thought to have built at least a hundred of these motte-and-bailey fortresses which remained the usual form of fortress for at least a hundred years after the Battle of Hastings, particularly in Ireland, Wales and Scotland, and a good many timber and earth fortresses were actually built in this last country as late as the twelfth and thirteenth centuries.

However, the advantages of stone fortresses were quickly discerned in England. The old wooden towers started to be demolished to make way for new stone buildings like the Round Tower at Windsor, and others at Lincoln, Lewis and Pickering. In the twelfth century enormous towers were put up in many parts of the country which subsequently in the sixteenth century came to be called Keeps, the name by which we constantly refer to them now, though it was never a term used by the Normans who called them simply 'great towers' or donjons. The latter part of the twelfth century became the era of the square keep, built of flint, rubble and stones mixed with mortar, and because these massive towers survived better than most other buildings, it is often thought that these were the standard type of medieval castles, although in fact, with the advancing designs of the next 300 years, they went out of fashion in a comparatively short time. They gave way first to the round keep which had clear military advantages over the square variety, then to various variations on both, and were finally dropped altogether in favour of great surrounding walls incorporating projecting towers or miniature keeps, encircling a courtyard with a more comfortable residence inside.

The years 1154 to 1216 incorporating the reigns of Henry II, Richard I and John were the great years of castlebuilding in England. By the end of this period the castles had become as much home as fortress as well as being the centre of local government, and open house to a constant stream of visitors. Naturally, a large staff was needed to run the place with any order. And this was headed by a steward or general manager, and included priests, almoners, clerks, tailors, sewing women, laundresses, a barber, 'wardrobers' (who took care not only of clothes, but of food, spices, wines, wax, jewels and silver plate), cooks, bakers, masons, carpenters, smiths, not to mention the ordinary servants and the defence garrison, all of whom had to be housed, clothed and fed.

But towards the end of the thirteenth century, the building of a completely new castle in England was already a rare event. There were at that period some 350 in existence and it became far more usual to improve on existing buildings, enlarging and strengthening their living quarters and defences.

Although Scotland was such a disorderly country for so long that castle-building went on there right up until the sixteenth and seventeenth centuries, almost two centuries longer than anywhere else. Nearly every landowner, however poor, was forced to build himself a simple keep or peel to protect his lands and his people, and today there are still numbers of these stone tower houses in existence all over the northern counties on both sides of the border ranging from the very simple to enormously ambitious fortresses like Lochleven in Kinross-shire or Warkworth in Northumberland.

The return of hundreds of mercenary soldiers in 1453 from the Hundred Years War brought the same sort of unrest to England,

which had in any case always been subject to a good deal of gory rivalry among the more powerful barons. These mercenaries, footloose and improvident, were only too ready to serve any lord for pay and plunder, and so the castle began to come into its own again as both refuge and base for attack. During these periods of unrest and civil war there was a consequent revival of castle-building, although they were on the whole simpler in plan and execution than their predecessors.

Two factors conspired to finally put an end to castles—at least as fortresses. One was the fact that Edward Stafford, 3rd Duke of Buckingham was executed by Henry VIII in the early 1500s for his temerity in building a great castle for himself at Thornbury in Gloucestershire. The other was the growing reliability of gunpowder. When heavy cannon became more efficient and their range exceeded a mile or more, it became obvious that the castle had outlived its military usefulness.

From this time on, any castles that were built were picturesque mansions rather than military fortresses. In Scotland, after peace had been declared with England and lairds had accumulated a comfortable and comforting share of church property, a number of them built in what came to be known as Scottish Baronial Style: castles like Glamis and Castle Fraser which, though undeniably Scottish, owed much to the French Chateaux with their complicated gables and turrets.

The cult of the ancient and

picturesque in the eighteenth and nineteenth centuries all over the British Isles, caused the erection of a number of so-called 'Gothick' castles and follies, which were really only large houses with battlements and towers added for romantic effect. Unfortunately, ruins were much sought after at this period and most of the early real castles were allowed to fall into neglect, their timbers and stone blocks sold or stolen, their walls crumbling into rubble.

Happily, just before it was altogether too late, the romantic appeal took a more practical form, and between Queen Victoria's reign and the Second World War, there were a number of people prepared to spend large sums on castle restoration. And these efforts, together with some splendid work by some enlightened local councils and the Ministry of Works, have preserved and often indeed, made practical for current living, examples which are now in their turn, inspiring yet further exercises.

I have introduced follies into this section because most of them are directly traceable to the romantic instincts that produced the Gothick castles, often themselves follies, of the last two centuries. They are sometimes castles or towers in miniature, sometimes fanciful recreations of castle appurtenances in the Gothick manner, and very often reconstructions of abbeys and hermitages, or just faked ruins. Whatever their final form, they are a unique part of the British tradition.

109

A Gothick Castle near Bath

Midford Castle, near Bath, built around 1775 by Henry Disney Roebuck, probably after a design by John Carter, is a romantic Gothick conceit, too serious in its plan to be a straight-forward folly, too late to be a castle proper.

It rears out of a cluster of beech trees above a steeply sloping park, and the story goes that it was built by a gambler who won a fortune on the ace of clubs and commemorated his coup by following suit and giving his house a trefoil plan. Certainly, the surrounding grounds also contain the ruins of a 'priory' which tradition connects with parties of bucks playing for fabulous stakes, but nevertheless, as the late Christopher Hussey remarked in *Country Life,* the feature which stamps the plan's resemblance to the ace of clubs, namely the imposing porch with its flanking turrets, which represents its stalk or foot, is, in fact, a later addition, built on by Charles Connelly, after he bought the property in 1810.

In any event, the plan though idiosyncratic, is simple enough, and makes a surprisingly practical house to run. In 1791, the historian Collinson remarked that 'The construction is singular, being in a triangular form with the angles rounded off and embattled at the top.' The three towers stand on a wide platform or sub-structure (echoes of the motte?) with a Bath stone parapet pierced with quatrefoils. In the old days, this subterranean area contained servants' quarters, stables, coach houses and a labyrinth of passages to connect it to the house proper. In the hands of the present owners, Michael and Isabel Briggs, this underworld has been sensibly converted to a flat, playrooms for the children and generous storage space.

As you enter the house proper through the Connelly porch, a large flagged hall opens on to a sitting-room-library on the left (originally the library), which takes care of one tower. A playroom, which was originally the drawing room is in the right hand tower, and the dining room fills the space in the third tower. The kitchen and other service rooms are now contained in a more recent addition just beyond. Through a door to the side of the hall, is the staircase which winds its way up to two more floors, each with the principal rooms contained in the three towers.

Beyond the castle is a stable quadrangle with Gothick pinnacles and Tudor chimneys, now converted into cottages, and to the North of this again, but adjoining it, is a chapel with a pretty Gothick greenhouse attached.

When Collinson wrote his history of Somerset in the late eighteenth century, he described Midford as even then having 'a very deep narrow sequestered glen' on the North and East sides of the house, 'the steep, narrow sides of which are clothed with fine coppice woods intersected with beautiful walks ornamented with flowering shrubs.' Nearly two hundred years later, the landscape has hardly changed except to become more romantic, more verdant and voluptuous. Roses

twist and clamber over the stone, carelessly clasping the crumbling ruins of priory and deserted chapel. And inside, the Briggs have consciously but subtly extended the cult of Gothick romance.

They have amassed a collection of Gothic furniture and decorated the rooms so that one immediately notices the extraordinary plasterwork of ceilings, the sash windows carried up to Gothick points and all the other architectural details. The current sitting room, retains the beautifully fitted original bookcases, veneered in mahogany and harewood, which repeat the shape of the windows, and the Briggs commissioned Lucy Bridgewater and Ed Gilbert to design the grapey-blue wallpaper with its tracery of purple which is unexpected but looks entirely right.

For the rest, the house is a comfortable mixture of oriental rugs, good strong colours, casual arrangements and occasional whimsical but successful touches like the organ pipes disguising a water tank in a passageway, the Gothick cane bedheads, and the tiny bathrooms cunningly fitted into the odd angle off some of the round bedrooms.

Above: *View of the hall*
Below: *The sitting room/library*

Above left and below: *Two bed-rooms*
Above: *Detail of passageway*

Carraigin Castle in County Galway

Looking at the soaring whitewashed keep of this early Gothick castle, standing on a particularly beautiful stretch of the eastern shore of Lough Corrib, it is difficult to realize that for 200 years and up until the 1970s, it had been a forlorn wreck open to the weather, its jagged walls shrouded by an enormous growth of ivy. Like a great many Irish medieval buildings, it had been abandoned by its owners in the eighteenth century in favour of a new Georgian mansion. Its roof had been stripped, hundreds of tons of stone had been removed, and it had been used as a quarry—though happily the quarrying had stopped before all traces of the character of the building had been lost, When Mr and Mrs Christopher Murphy, the present owners, came across it, most of the parapets, half the tower and the cornerstones of the building had disappeared, whilst the windows and doors, once lined with finely chiselled mouldings, were reduced to gaping holes.

Undeterred, the Murphy's saw the possibilities there were for restoration and determined to buy it. It took weeks to clear away the debris from the two main floors, and more weeks to strip the ivy and dig out the roots from the broken tops of the walls. Because of the depopulation of the countryside, large quantities of secondhand building stone were available nearby and in all some 300 tons were obtained from an abandoned schoolhouse and three small cottages. In fact the stone matched so well, that the masons were con-vinced they were only replacing material that had been removed from the castle during its quarry days, some 200 years earlier.

Christopher Murphy insisted on the same techniques of stone-laying, corbelling and arching as would have been used by the original builders, and slowly the castle was restored, its outside walls crenellated in the manner of the thirteenth century, and its corner tower raised from a 25ft. stump to a full 50ft. Inside, too, the restoration is as near the original interior as is compatible with reasonably comfortable twentieth century living. The great hall is still the principal room and one can still look up to the heavy oak beams of the roof, although the original open hearth has been replaced by a fireplace and a chimney of roughly fifteenth century design, to obviate the necessity of smoke having to escape through a hole in the roof. Now, overlooking the hall, is a large gallery which forms one of the two double bedrooms. Underneath, occupying the other third of the first floor, are the main bedroom, a small bathroom and a little stair well from which a stone staircase now runs up to the gallery.

From the opposite corner of the hall, a wall passage leads into the tower, which now houses the kitchen at first floor level, and on the second floor, up a flight of winding stone steps, a single bedroom. From this room, as well as from the gallery, one can go out onto the wall walk—a broad path right around the foot of the roof, protected on the outside by a tall crenellated parapet wall. And fom this wall walk, another flight of stone steps leads up to the flat roof of the tower, from where there is a spectacular view over the lough to the Connemara and Partry Mountains.

The ground floor with its dark vaulted rooms, was never originally intended for living accommodation, but has now been adapted to provide two large children's dormitories, another bathroom and an entrance hall. The windows have been restored on a much larger scale than the originals, and these, together with the surprisingly bright light by the lake shore and the reflective qualities of the whitewash, ensure that the area is now adequately lit.

Furniture and furnishings have been kept very simple. The stone floors are rush-matted, and the long low arches on the ground floor which support the vaulting along the centre of the building, have been adapted to provide built-in cupboards. Outside, an area of meadow around the walls is kept in trim by sheep, and the Murphys have started a plantation of mixed indigenous trees and plant to surround the castle with all kinds of hardwood, softwood and shrubs. It is a marvellous place to escape to, and a monument to enterprise.

Far right: *Great Hall*
Below: *Elevation*
Right: *Details of stonework*

A Norman Keep in Westmorland

David Lockart-Smith and his wife have always lived in ancient houses, but when, fearful of the encroaching urbanization of the South, they decided to look for a ruin which they could slowly restore in the border country between the Northern counties and Scotland, they could not have dreamt of finding something so exactly as they had imagined, or so perfectly situated.

Partly the remnants of a Norman keep, much of it medieval, it looms, a dramatic, great grey mass out of a wild stretch of country where the only sounds are primitively agricultural, classically rural: the bleating of sheep, an occasional cock.

It is going to be an arduous task to turn it into the sort of living space that they require for it has been derelict for years, but it seemed well worth photographing as an example of what can be tackled.

'Primitively agricultural, classically rural'

A Gothick Folly in Cambridgeshire

The Cambridgeshire-Hertfordshire-Essex borders are rich in eighteenth century follies, which are nevertheless still rare to come by. When Dudley Poplak, an interior designer, was offered one, albeit in the last stages of decrepitude, he negotiated for it with enthusiasm.

Built of flintstone in local idiom, it sits in a commanding position on a hill just by a ruined windmill in a highly picturesque-grouping. Mr Poplak entirely replanned the interior to make it a comfortable, practical, beautifully detailed house, that can be left and taken up again, at will. Although full of rural detail: flagged stone floors, old bricks, rush matting, and clearly battling against the wind and hostile elements, it still manages to be extremely sophisticated.

The Gothicism is carefully complimented by eighteenth-century and early nineteenth century furniture; by appropriate fabrics; subtle colouring, and cunningly graduated, and well-chosen objects. The flagged entrance hall turns left into sitting room and bedroom, right into kitchen, dining room and guest bedroom. Space, though scanty, is carefully allotted and distributed, so that the whole building seems very light and spacious, and every available surface is permeated with an enviable sense of arrangement, that thoroughly compliments the original inception of the folly.

Having finished the main house to his satisfaction, Mr Poplak now has great plans for turning the windmill into extra entertaining rooms.

Left: *Detail of a bedroom*
Above: *Detail of arrangements*
Below: *Corner of the drawing room*

Above: *The hall*
Below and right: *Bedroom details*

Glenveagh Castle in County Donegal

Glenveagh Castle, built in the 1870s on what must be one of the most beautiful wild landscapes in Ireland—a country not unrenowned after all, for its landscape —was originally designed as a square Gothick keep by I. T. Trench, for his cousin, Mr John Adair. The round tower was apparently an afterthought. The great granite masses rear up from a promontory jutting in Lough Veagh, surrounded by rare and exotic plants which thrive in the shelter of the rocks and trees, and in June the air is full of a quite extraordinary fragrance from the rhododendrons and the azaleas.

Mrs Adair was an American heiress, Cornelia Wadsworth of Geneseo, and was in the great tradition of American hostesses of that era. Edward VII sent her over a stag from Windsor to help start the herd of deer, which, now, a hundred years later, have expanded to between some eight and nine hundred. In 1929 the property was bought by another American, Professor Arthur Kingsley Porter, a distinguished archaeologist and Professor of Fine Arts at Harvard University. And in 1938 it was bought by its current owner and its third American proprietor, Mr Henry McIlhenny of Philadelphia, who was for thirty years Curator of Decorative Arts at the Philadelphia Museum, of which he is now vice-president.

In spite of Glenveagh's rather forbidding aspect, it is, inside, one of the most comfortable, civilised and idiosyncratic of houses with all the opulence of the best of Edwardiana. The rounded windows with their plate-glass and polished brass fittings, the blazing turf fires in every grate, the Victorian paintings by Landseer, Ansdell, Buckner and AE (George Russell), the rich, clear colours, the handsome eighteenth century Irish furniture mixed with the odd piece of Victoriana, the antlers everywhere (some 150 deer are slaughtered every year on the estate), make of the inside an extraordinarily nostalgic experience.

The entrance hall with its *coquillage* decoration of sea shells embedded in plaster, is punctuated by antlers every few yards. The red sitting room with its great long white sofa and splendidly practical small drinks table from Hong Kong embedded in the upholstery, its lion and unicorn mirror, and white red-bordered curtains, is a particularly good nineteenth century room. The drawing room—the Green Room—is really the Grand Salon, with its delicate Georgian furniture, its French chintz and its rugs woven specially to match the chintz in Portugal. The music room has tartan walls and a marvellous antler candelabra. Bathrooms are solidly comfortable and luxurious.

Outside, all the outbuildings are castellated, their doors painted a Tuscan green, the estate colour. Mr McIlhenny has made a statue garden, a rose garden, a wild garden; and a flight of a hundred steps leads up to a hillside vantage point overlooking the mountains and the vast stretch of the lough.

Right: *The profile of Glenveagh Castle seen across Lough Reagh.*

Top left: *The dining room*
Top right: *The hall*
Above: *The music room*
Right: *The green drawing room*

Top left: *The red room*
Top right: *Another view of the red room*
Left: *A bathroom*
Above: *A bedroom*

Scottish Baronial on the River Spey

In a way, this house belonging to the Hon. Anthony and Mrs Samuel is the epitome of Scottish Baronial. Mr Samuel bought it after having rented it for some time for the fishing, and was delighted when it actually came on the market. It has everything to commend it: marvellous situation on a hill overlooking the River Spey; impeccable references going back to 1740; an extraordinary cantilevered staircase, door cases and architraves ascribed to one of the brothers Adam, and above all, space.

Wandering around the house, it is obvious that it owes allegiance to all sorts of periods from pure Norman to High Victorian, and it has been furnished and decorated (by David Hicks) with a panache that is rare in holiday homes, though it is clear that the building deserves it.

In fact, the decoration, though arresting, is really quite simple, and is designed to throw forward the lavish plasterwork and mouldings. The drawing room is painted a clear cerulean blue, with plain white curtains and green and white covered seating, and a round table in the bay is covered in a vivid green and red fabric. The dining room is altogether a darker blue, with a floor length tablecloth in blues and greens on an oriental carpet. And the main bedroom is all pink walls and pink and white chintz for the four poster bed.

The clear colours against the strong grey stone of the outer walls; the tumbling Scottish scenery; the towers, and curving walls, and semi-fortress-like-appearance, are all highly romantic factors.

Left: *Cantilevered staircase attributed to Adam*
Below: *The drawing room attributed to David Hicks*

Above: *Dining room*
Right: *Bedroom*

The Modern House

There is a disappointing lack of good new houses in this country and even fewer good new houses that can truly be called second homes. This is partly due to the plethora of tempting old houses still extant; partly to high land prices and building costs; and partly because designing individual houses is notoriously unprofitable for British architects. But mostly, it is because of prejudice against new forms, so that those individuals determined enough to commission and build, are often harassed relentlessly by philistine local authorities on the one side (for whom a house can clearly only mean a brick box with a pitched roof), and on the other by lack of financial support from short-sighted building societies. The sad thing is that incipient builders are often deterred by neighbourly prejudice as well; deflected by the sort of conservationists to whom any modern building, whatever its merits, is necessarily an abhorrence. And there have been notable occasions when planning permission to build has finally and reluctantly been given simply because it was conceded impossible for anyone else casually to see the offending house. There is scarcely a person who has built a private house in this country without some alarming tale of prejudice to relate.

In spite of all this there are growing numbers of determined people prepared to undergo the months of almost certain trouble with the local authority, the architect, the builder, the mains Water Board and the Electricity Board,

'. . . to build a house can also be a rare and absorbing pleasure . . .'

and more months, even years, in looking for their perfect site in woods, on hillsides, by rivers or lakes. There are of course the people who have the chance of building on inherited land or land they own already, but even so, anyone who decides to build can almost inevitably look forward to a frustrating time—though there may be some consolation in the fact that it is possibly fractionally less difficult now, than over the preceding decade.

This being said—or grumbled, the fact remains that to build a house can also be a rare and absorbing pleasure. To order more or less exactly what you want within the limits of your income; to plan position, angle and comfort; to discuss timbers, finishes, sophistications; to nurture, cajole, conjure, all these are satisfying and fulfilling experiences.

Obviously, to plan and build a holiday or part-time house so to speak, involves a rather different set of design criteria than a permanent home. Living space should be at a maximum and then elastic; sleeping spaces should be numerous (unless you are hermitic which is possible) but minimal and none the less well-planned for that; and kitchens should be large enough to eat in, or barely divided from the main living area. Open plan which is often now rejected in more formal buildings, is rather to be encouraged in informal ones, and the whole should be formulated to be maintained with the minimum of upkeep and domestic chores.

Furnishing and decoration can be a great deal less inhibited than in a full-time house. The most practical flooring for casual country or waterside houses is undoubtedly some sort of tiling or brick, scattered with rugs. Natural surfaces: brick, wood, stone, granite, marble, appear to advantage. So do bright warm colours, since an unbroken mass of white rarely appears at its best in the soft light of Britain and Ireland.

Furniture can be idiosyncratic, knock-down, sturdy, expendable. So it can in any house, but there are certain types of casual furniture produced nowadays: the Sacco and Lay-about chairs for example, the blow-ups and the expandable foam, not to mention all the other foam seating, and the over-sized cushions that are peculiarly useful for determinedly relaxed living, and on the whole, much cheaper; a distinct advantage when building costs almost always manage to be inexplicably double the estimates. And it is nice not to be tramelled by a building, not to have to reverence its age or proportions, not to be dictated to in any way.

The first problem to be overcome when planning to build is to find the right architect. Engaging someone because you have seen and admired his work whether *in situ*, or in a book, magazine or newspaper, is one way; personal recommendation by a friend another; going to the local authority architect a third, and consulting a local Professor of Architecture if the site happens to be near a University a fourth. On the whole it is best not to commission an architect friend, unless you are quite sure of the strength of your friendship—although conversely, many architects originally called in as strangers have become life long friends with their clients.

Having gathered together a list of possibles, take a good look at some of their work. Satisfied clients will rarely mind their houses being looked over, and the architects themselves will always make appointments and furnish photographs. Do not be afraid of ruthlessly searching out the person who will suit you best. If you still feel no rapport with an architect after two or three meetings, it is much better to dismiss him tactfully and start again.

There is absolutely nothing to stop you employing an architect from quite the opposite end of the country to your chosen site if you think his work is what you want, or from another country altogether for

that matter, if you are prepared to spend the money for his travelling expenses. But do remember that the advantages of a local architect include familiarity with the foibles of the local inspector and planning committee, as well as better supervision of the contractor's work and a considerably lower expense account. One compromise is to employ your chosen architect as the consultant as it were, and the local firm as the general practitioners, although this is a more expensive ploy, and all parties need to exert a certain amount of tact.

For the rest, the procedure is much the same as that which I have outlined in the section on conversions. However much trust you have in your architect, you should pay as regular visits to the site as time and distance allows. For all his worth, he will not be a mind-reader and in the best-planned operations there are always hitches and problems for which in the last resort only you can give a decision. When it comes to the crunch after all, the only person who is wholeheartedly dedicated to guarding your interests is yourself.

Of the houses in this section, only one is designed by an architect for himself and his wife, also an architect, the rest are for large families or families with constant visitors. All are on totally disparate sites, and all have finished up with totally disparate design solutions.

A Courtyard House on the East Anglian Coast

The Cadbury-Browns are both architects and both have a subtle eye for arrangement, detail, space and texture. The small house they have built for themselves in Aldeburgh, on the Suffolk coast is, to me, at any rate, a classic of its kind. Built of warm grey, handmade Marks Tey bricks, it has been planned to take advantage of every nuance of light from the unpredictable, ever-changing East Anglian sky.

Externally, it is built around three sides of an enclosed courtyard which traps every last ray of sun, and is now burgeoning with plants and climbers and foliage of all sorts. The other side fronts onto a wild garden with meandering paths cut through the long grass and the tower of the church in the background.

Inside, white plastered walls are finished with a metal bead which obviates the necessity for normal skirtings or cornices. Windows and doors are designed to hinge right back so that one can see from space to space without interruption. Floors are made from blue-black quarry tiles, and one of the special successes of the house with its taut design, are the shafts of light let in here and there from windows cut into the roof; windows which not only let in an extra dimension of light, but allow anyone lying in bed, for example, to get splendid vignettes of the trees and sky outside.

The spaces, too are very interesting. A large living room, with a raised platform at one end, has a built-up skirting at platform level all around which also leads into a

built-in stove making an admirably warm sitting place in the winter. In the bedrooms, furniture is kept to a minimum, and beds kept low to the floor, so that nothing detracts from the sense of space, and light, and the particular attention to texture in the building itself.

All the same, there are always lovely, simple, extraneous details, like a bunch of cow parsley spraying out from a plain glass jar all caught in the light against the white of the wall; a vase of grasses set on some vivid blue Arts and Crafts Movement tiles on a bedroom floor; a group of glass set in front of a propped-up panel of mirrorlite, itself set to further catch and exaggerate the light.

The house evolved slowly, mostly because both partners were so busy, they had little time to spend on their own projects. But it has also been evolved most lovingly. It is rare to see a house with such purity of line.

Above: *One end of the living room*
Right: *Another view of the living room*

Two bedrooms

A Single-storey House in a Suffolk Sailing Village

The Vannecks have almost always been an East Anglian family, and one branch or another has owned Wyatt's great Heveningham Hall until it was recently taken over by the Government. Therefore it seems particularly apt that Group Captain the Hon. Peter Vanneck, who was brought up in Heveningham, should have commissioned a modern house, comparatively near his old home, for himself, his wife and daughter, from Peter Moro, FRIBA.

Mr. Moro's brief was to build a simple, easily run house in the Suffolk sailing village where the Vannecks keep their boat. The garden and living quarters have been admirably, comfortably and casually integrated in an unpretentious way, and the finished product, now a decade or so old, wears extremely well.

A Wood House in an Old Garden in Oxfordshire

The house shown here on the Berkshire–Oxfordshire borders was built in a well-wooded and wildish old garden which slopes down in terraces to a lake, and was originally the home of Sir Arthur Evans, the archaeologist who discovered Knossos in Crete. The decrepit and not very beautiful old house had been pulled down in 1950, and the garden had waited some 20 years dormant, untended but still luxuriant, for a new house to be substituted.

When they acquired the site, William and Celia Goodhart briefed their architect, Hal Moggridge of Colvin and Moggridge, to design a weekend or holiday house with about six bedrooms which would be just as practical for year-round living. It had to be easy to run, and it had to take advantage of the views and terrain. It had to be a house in which children could bang about with impunity, and at the same time be satisfactorily separated from adults whenever it was thought to be judicious. And above all it had to be an exciting piece of architecture on more than one level.

Mr. Moggridge's solution to these basic precepts, and many other practical details suggested by his clients, is interesting. The house takes advantage of the sloping ground with its long shape which soars upwards at the southern elevation so that the living room at the top floor, the main bedroom at first floor level, and the playroom beneath are all built on the side of the hill.

As you walk into the house the large dining room and kitchen are set to the north. A diagonal hallway which provides access from one end of the building to the other was so shaped in order to avoid the appearance of being a dark and narrow corridor. The family bedrooms and bathrooms and a study are also on this floor, and a curving concrete staircase leads down to the spacious playroom, and up to the still more spacious sitting room and guest room area. The floors are reinforced concrete, cork tiled in the kitchen and dining room areas, brown wool cord-carpeted in the others, so that noise transmission between levels is minimised. And the whole house is carried by pre-cast concrete columns visible along all side walls. These are tied together at each floor level by a horizontal beam along the outside wall, cast with the floor and shaped to contain heating elements and pipe runs—a graceful, distinctive and uniting element for the building.

All the living areas—dining room, kitchen, and especially the sitting room, are large and well-proportioned. In a way it was a problem to decorate them to the distinguished standards of the architecture. The owners managed the task with equal distinction, for furnishings and colours are idiosyncratic without being disturbing and in just the right proportion of old and new, so that the house, either inside or out, could in no way be dated exactly.

Overleaf: *Rear elevation*
Far left: *Front door and side elevation*
Left: *Staircase and main corridor*
Below: *One end of the sitting room*

Right: *The dining room*
Far right: *A guest bedroom*
Below: *Another view of the sitting room from the stair well*

An Old Site Re-used in Fife

It is always useful to be able to build on an old site with all the attendant advantages of existing landscaping and outbuildings. And Lord and Lady Balniel made the best of their opportunities when they asked Trevor Dannatt to design a holiday house for them on the ruins of old Pitcorthie house in Fife, which would take into account the magnificent views across the village of Eric to the sea, as well as the existing courtyard and group of old buildings.

Mr Dannatt's plan came up to their expectations. The front entrance up steps to a terrace and from thence into a lobby, is approached through a courtyard bound by the original reconstructed walls and outbuildings on the East and North sides (which have been made into children's playroom, garages and a sheltered terrace). On the West, there is a new caretaker's cottage, and to the South is the house itself, the main body of which is oriented to the South, with a living room block looking West.

The house is really very simple. It is built on one floor only, with the circulation and living space surrounding a core of service rooms which get their light from high clerestory windows facing South. The entire South side of the house is glazed, with just behind, a six foot wide strip of gallery connecting all the rooms. At one end, is the dining room, study and main bedroom and these last two rooms can be cut off from the dining room and through gallery by sliding doors. At the other, are two long, narrow

bedrooms—each with four bunks for children—and a guest room, through the study can also be made into an extra bedroom if needed.

The living room block is quite different in character. A high pitched ceiling slopes down to windows overlooking the terraces and garden, and is approached by steps from the rest of the living space. A large fireplace with exposed flue rises up through the highest part of the room and gives a splendid focal point to a spacious room, which is also visually subdivided by a cross-shaped pillar which partly supports the roof.

The kitchen, too, is an interesting room. During the day it is always full of light from the clerestory windows, but equally, an outsize hatch opening into the dining room, enables anyone working in there to get full advantage from the extra high and splendid rural views through the dining room windows. At one end of the kitchen is a full width stainless steel top with built-in sinks and hob units, in the middle is a working top with good storage beneath and another sink, and at the far end is a special children's area.

External finishes are grey stone and wood; internal finishes are white-painted rough cast walls, white-painted plaster board, and wood floors and ceilings. Furnishings are very simple and colourful —a mixture of Habitat stock and old pine and cane. And there is a good collection of rugs on the floor.

It has all been beautifully planned.

Views of exterior, dining room and kitchen

The sitting room and two bedrooms

A House on Beaulieu River

When Mr and Mrs Robert Garrett decided to build a house for themselves on the river at Beaulieu, they asked Michael Pattrick, who had built several houses in the area, to design it for them. It was a happy choice of architect, and a felicitous choice of site, because they managed to find land surrounded by woodland, yet within yards of a wide stretch of the river, and Mr Pattrick, by excavating a series of ponds, managed to make the water come almost up, indeed at some points, right up, to the house itself. And these ponds, now full of fish, and rushes, here banked with lawn, there with a great tangle of undergrowth, here again, more formally, with duckboarding and brick, are constantly invaded by ducks and moorhens and dragon flies, so that the view is never for one moment static.

The house itself, started off by being a single pavilion with a glassed front, mostly consisting of large living room, kitchen and bedroom space. But gradually over the years, it has grown wings, which angle off and from separate courtyards of their own, so that now the house appears to spread generously and effortlessly over a vast area and can comfortably accommodate endless guests. In short it is a perfect weekend house.

The Garretts now have their own bedroom wing at right angles to the original block and joined to it by a wide corridor with a duck-boarded loggia in front leading straight to the water. If at any time, they are guestless, they can live very comfortably shut off from all the rest of the new additions which have their own separate existence. The structure is white painted concrete, wood and an endless series of full-length windows which open out onto the garden and water, and it is geared to take every possible advantage of the outdoors.

Indeed it is difficult to define an area where house ends and outdoors begins since house and landscaping are so carefully integrated. And the furnishing and decoration of the house is kept as simple and unaffected as possible so that nothing detracts from the ever-changing vista of ponds and trees and river.

Below: *View from sitting room over the pond*

154

Below: *View from main bedroom over the pond*

A Hilltop House on the Sussex Downs

Mr and Mrs Duncan Guthrie had owned at various times three houses in the country before they finally decided to build for themselves. In fact they had two houses in much the same area in Sussex: an Elizabethan cottage; then a house they inherited from an aunt that she had built in 1924; and penultimately, a converted Congregational chapel in Hertfordshire. But they had always had a great preference for Sussex, and a particular preference for the village of Amberley. To this end, they bought a house perched right on the ridge overlooking miles of the North Downs with a largish garden because it was exactly the site that they wanted. They then got planning permission to build, and sold off the original house.

The new house, an uncompromising single storey building of concrete block, wood and glass, was designed by Lattimore, Morgan and Sharp to a brief for an open plan house with one double, three single bedrooms, good living space, and the proviso that every room must take full advantage of the view.

At first, the local people were full of indignation about the plans, although the Guthries were greatly sustained by the fact that the County Council at Chichester approved of the project. But in spite of the original strong objections from the village, the house is now fully accepted and even rather liked. . . .

All the rooms open off a gallery-like corridor, well-planted and glassed, which runs the whole length of the house. And although the building is deliberately stark and simple outside, it is full of carefully-considered colour and thoughtful arrangement within. Bedrooms are kept to a minimum of space, but are none the less comfortable for that, and the living, cooking, eating area with its warm brick floors and eclectic choice of furniture and furnishings are easy and casual.

Left: *Living room*
Above: *The kitchen and two views
of the long hallway*

Bibliography

THE ENGLISH COTTAGE by H. Batsford and Charles Fry (*Batsford*)

THE TRUTH ABOUT COTTAGES by John Woodforde (*Routledge & Kegan Paul*)

THE CHARM OF THE ENGLISH VILLAGE by Ditchfield S. R. Jones (*Batsford*)

THE PATTERN OF ENGLISH BUILDING by Alec Clifton-Taylor (*Batsford*)

CASTLES by R. J. Unstead (*A. & C. Black Ltd.*)

ARCHITECTURE IN BRITAIN TODAY by Michael Webb (*Country Life*)

DOING UP A HOUSE by Mary Gilliatt (*Bodley Head*)